Choosing the Right Legal Form of Business:

The Complete Guide to Becoming a Sole Proprietor, Partnership, LLC, or Corporation

By PK Fontana

Foreword by Kyle J. Lavender, Cofounder
INCFILE.COM LLC

9/10 LAO 4/10 - 2Ⓒ

Choosing the Right Legal Form of Business: The Complete Guide to Becoming a Sole Proprietor, Partnership, LLC, or Corporation

Copyright © 2010 Atlantic Publishing Group, Inc.
1405 SW 6th Avenue • Ocala, Florida 34471 • Phone 800-814-1132 • Fax 352-622-1875
Web site: www.atlantic-pub.com • E-mail: sales@atlantic-pub.com
SAN Number: 268-1250

Library of Congress Cataloging-in-Publication Data

Fontana, P. K.
  Choosing the right legal form of business : the complete guide to becoming a sole proprietor, partnership, LLC, or corporation / by P.K. Fontana.
    p. cm.
  Includes bibliographical references and index.
  ISBN-13: 978-1-60138-301-3 (alk. paper)
  ISBN-10: 1-60138-301-0 (alk. paper)
  1. Business enterprises--Law and legislation--United States. I. Title.
  KF1355.F66 2010
  346.73'065--dc22

                     2009048314

Printed in the United States

PROJECT MANAGER: Erin Everhart • eeverhart@atlantic-pub.com
PEER REVIEWER: Marilee Griffin • mgriffin@atlantic-pub.com
INTERIOR DESIGN: Holly Gibbs • hgibbs@atlantic-pub.com
ASSISTANT EDITOR: Angela Pham • apham@atlantic-pub.com
COVER DESIGN: Meg Buchner • meg@megbuchner.com
BACK COVER DESIGN: Jackie Miller • millerjackiej@gmail.com

Printed on Recycled Paper

We recently lost our beloved pet "Bear," who was not only our best and dearest friend but also the "Vice President of Sunshine" here at Atlantic Publishing. He did not receive a salary but worked tirelessly 24 hours a day to please his parents. Bear was a rescue dog that turned around and showered myself, my wife, Sherri, his grandparents Jean, Bob, and Nancy, and every person and animal he met (maybe not rabbits) with friendship and love. He made a lot of people smile every day.

We wanted you to know that a portion of the profits of this book will be donated to The Humane Society of the United States. *–Douglas & Sherri Brown*

The human-animal bond is as old as human history. We cherish our animal companions for their unconditional affection and acceptance. We feel a thrill when we glimpse wild creatures in their natural habitat or in our own backyard.

Unfortunately, the human-animal bond has at times been weakened. Humans have exploited some animal species to the point of extinction.

The Humane Society of the United States makes a difference in the lives of animals here at home and worldwide. The HSUS is dedicated to creating a world where our relationship with animals is guided by compassion. We seek a truly humane society in which animals are respected for their intrinsic value, and where the human-animal bond is strong.

Want to help animals? We have plenty of suggestions. Adopt a pet from a local shelter, join The Humane Society and be a part of our work to help companion animals and wildlife. You will be funding our educational, legislative, investigative and outreach projects in the U.S. and across the globe.

Or perhaps you'd like to make a memorial donation in honor of a pet, friend or relative? You can through our Kindred Spirits program. And if you'd like to contribute in a more structured way, our Planned Giving Office has suggestions about estate planning, annuities, and even gifts of stock that avoid capital gains taxes.

Maybe you have land that you would like to preserve as a lasting habitat for wildlife. Our Wildlife Land Trust can help you. Perhaps the land you want to share is a backyard— that's enough. Our Urban Wildlife Sanctuary Program will show you how to create a habitat for your wild neighbors.

So you see, it's easy to help animals. And The HSUS is here to help.

THE HUMANE SOCIETY
OF THE UNITED STATES.

2100 L Street NW • Washington, DC 20037 • 202-452-1100
www.hsus.org

Dedication

As always, my work is dedicated to Fred, Rudy, and Katie, with deep appreciation to Clara and J.E.

Acknowledgements

Thanks go out to my editor, Erin Everhart, for patiently answering my many questions about this project and for providing such constructive and timely feedback. And thanks to Amanda Miller, who gave me this opportunity.

Thanks also to the many people who contributed their own stories, found in the case studies throughout this book. Many of those who contributed to the case studies have experienced business failure as well as success. We are grateful that they were willing to share all of their experiences so that others may learn the valuable lessons that they did along the way.

A special thanks to the organizations and individuals who spend their time helping others who are launching businesses or who are developing growth plans for their businesses. There are many valuable resources, many of which are listed in this book, to help guide you in starting and growing your business.

To those for whom this book is written, thank you for reading it. I trust it will be a helpful guide to help you get started on the right foot in your new business venture.

Table of Contents

Chapter 3: Sole Proprietorships   49

Chapter 4: Partnerships   57

Chapter 5: LLCs   87

Chapter 6: Corporations   123

Foreword

When it comes to starting and running a business, the selection of the type of business structure for your company is one of the first and most important decisions you will make. Many up-and-coming entrepreneurs find themselves unsure as to which structure is the most suitable for their needs, and the topic can seem intimidating, even overwhelming, to some. In addition, once the proper business structure for your company has been determined, the company still needs to be properly formed and operated. Many individuals simply have no idea where to begin or where to turn for good information. In her book *Choosing the Right Legal Form of Business: The Complete Guide to Becoming a Sole Proprietor, Partnership, LLC, or Corporation*, PK Fontana takes the subject well in hand and presents a great deal of important and relevant information in a logical, organized, and highly readable fashion. Anyone, regardless of their level of business experience, will have their knowledge and understanding of the topic greatly enhanced after reading this book.

Many people think that setting up a company is too complex for them to handle and that it may even require the services of an attorney. Nothing could be further from the truth. With this book as a resource, anyone will be well-equipped to handle just about any issue that arises. With this book at your side, you will find that the process is far less daunting than you thought — and well within your grasp. You will learn what documents need to be prepared, where and when they need to be filed, and the ongoing compliance requirements, both internal and external, to keep your company up-to-date and in good standing. You will also gain the necessary knowledge and understanding required to decide if and when it is appropriate to consult with an attorney.

This book is quite impressive in its breadth and depth. Of course, it covers all the requirements to form the four business structures in a detailed, step-by-step fashion, but it also covers topics that many other books only give cursory treatment — or no treatment at all. For example, the sections regarding the sale, conversion, or dissolution of your company contain hard-to-come-by information, and the coverage of tax and legal issues alone is worth the cover price many times over. Additionally, it has an excellent discussion of how to handle operating in more than one state and why and when you would need to register in other states. This is a very important topic but, unfortunately, one that is seldom addressed. The book concludes with several case studies that provide real-world examples and insights.

As the cofounder of INCFILE.COM, one of the largest online incorporation services in the United States, I have been involved in the formation of more than 30,000 businesses. It has been very rewarding to help people on their way down the entrepreneurial path, and understanding the various business structures is a vital part of that journey. The decision as to which type of structure to use for a given company will affect almost every aspect of the business going forward, and the importance of this decision should not be underestimated or taken lightly. I found the information in this book extremely helpful, and I believe everyone will find it an invaluable resource, from the budding entrepreneur to the most seasoned of business veterans.

Best wishes in all of your business endeavors.

> Kyle J. Lavender
> Incorporation Specialist
> Cofounder, INCFILE.COM LLC
> kyle@incfile.com
> **www.incfile.com**
> 888-INC-FILE

Introduction

Whether you are planning to start a business or you are already in business and considering changing the appropriate structure, you have taken the right first step by picking up this book. *Choosing the Right Legal Form of Business* will guide you through all the steps you need to determine the legal structure that will work best for you and your business in terms of taxes, liability, paperwork, and others you may need to involve in the operations of your business.

Before you start a business, you must be aware of the different types of business formations available. Each has its own features, benefits, tax structures, organization, and management. Each affects how you will raise money, protect your legal rights, file and pay taxes, and operate your business. Your choice of business entity is as important as the people you hire, the marketing plan you implement, or the financial records you maintain. Therefore, it is imperative to not only be familiar with the fact that there are different types of business formations, but to understand each of them completely. Even if you decide to hire a lawyer, you should be informed about the ramifications of the different business entities so you can ask intelligent questions and carry on a discourse with your attorney.

But is having a lawyer necessary to start your business? Startup costs for a business can be great, and you may not want to spend the money. While that choice is, of course, entirely up to you, this book can help you save money on attorney fees by providing thorough discussions of the available options. The added security of an attorney providing legal advice is a plus, but it is possible to cut costs and time spent at an attorney's office by doing your homework and learning as much as possible about the legal and financial elements of various types of business entities.

You should read and learn about all of the legal forms of business, even if you may not need the information now. Business structures often change as the business grows. You may start your business as a sole proprietorship but decide to convert it to a corporation at some later date. In this case, you need to be informed about both sole proprietorships and corporations. Also, you may start your business as a partnership, but later your partner may want to get out of the business. In this case, you would have to know how to properly dissolve a partnership. Your choice of business entity affects you and your business now and well into the future as your business expands and prospers. Your decision is a business strategy. Therefore, the more information you have, the better off you will be as your business changes and grows.

In addition to providing details regarding the legal ramifications of the various business formations, this book will discuss the non-legal issues you need to consider before you start your business. These issues range from the simple (ease of setup) to the more complex (taxation). Examine each type of business entity to find the right one for your needs — and those of your new business — with these considerations in mind:

- **Ease of setup:** Reviewing the potential complications involved in setting up the business.

- **Preliminary costs:** Determining whether the costs are excessive or reasonable for your particular circumstances as you plan the launch of your new business.

- **Liability:** Deciding how much liability you and your business may face and how you can protect yourself.

- **Filings:** Understanding what needs to be filed and when — and with which entity.

- **Meetings:** Knowing when to hold meetings and who has to be involved in your meetings.

- **Formalities:** Understanding other requirements involved in the business legal form you have chosen, such as reports or notices.

- **Life of business:** Determining how you will handle your business — or how your family will handle your business — if it is dissolved, faces bankruptcy, or experiences the loss of the owner.

- **Stock:** Examining the need and the ability to sell portions of ownership of your business.

- **Raising capital:** Examining the ability to raise capital through investors or financial institutions.

- **Taxes:** Understanding the tax implications of the various legal forms of business, particularly the corporation and partnership.

- **Mixing funds:** Understanding when the business is considered a separate entity and when owners can mix business and personal monies.

- **Registering for foreign business:** Deciding whether you need to register your business in another state if you do business there.

- **State laws:** Understanding state laws that may differ for your particular form of business entity.

- **Members:** Determining how many members your legal form of business entity requires.

Our discussion of the administrative issues to consider when choosing a business formation then leads us to a discussion of the formations themselves. What are they? What are their legal ramifications? How will this choice affect the future of the business? This section provides the answers to those questions through a discourse of how we define each one, together with their respective advantages and disadvantages. You will learn about sole proprietorships, partnerships, corporations, and limited liability companies, better known as LLCs, as well as a few other, more specialized types of business entities, such as limited partnerships and S corporations.

If you are a budding entrepreneur, you will find this book extremely helpful as a guide through the initial stages of starting a business. We will cover the basics of choosing a name and location, dealing with taxes and finances, and choosing the type of business entity that works best for you and your business. Even if you have already formed a business and chosen a business entity, this book will prove beneficial to you. You will find tips on how to save on taxes, file your paperwork, and transfer ownership. *Chapter 7 will discuss how you can convert your present business entity to another business entity.* The book contains information on the tax structures of each business entity together with the applicable federal and tax laws governing such entities. It also contains invaluable information and examples on the legal and financial ramifications of limited liability pro- tection — an important concept when you are a business owner seeking asset protection.

Finally, as an added bonus, the book contains case stud- ies — mini-interviews — with professionals in the field and business owners who speak from their own experience about the importance of choosing the right business entity. The subjects of these case studies have either started their own business or worked with others to help them start a business. They speak from their extensive experience about the lessons they have learned and how that may help you as you proceed with your business plans.

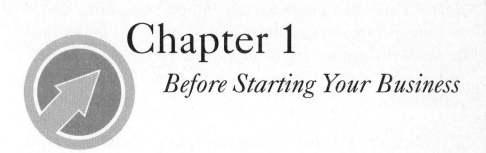

Chapter 1

Before Starting Your Business

New businesses fail primarily due to lack of planning and preparation — about 50 percent of all small businesses fail within the first five years, according to the Small Business Administration (SBA). This chapter covers the important administrative issues you will need to consider as you are planning your new business that will help ensure success. Although the information found in this chapter will not necessarily directly impact your choice of legal form for your business, it will impact your chances for success as you plan the first stages of starting your new business. The steps provided here will enable you to develop a solid foundation for a business that will grow and prosper.

Location

Early in your business planning process, you must decide where the business should be located. A growing business trend in today's work world is the home-based business. Many entrepreneurs are choosing to keep their overhead low by operating from a home office, rather than spending money on office rent. Advances in technology such as the

Internet, Web conferences, and other communications innovations have made it easy to operate a business — including interacting with clients — from a home-based office. With online technology, you can easily connect with clients across the country and across the globe from your computer.

If you decide to lease or purchase commercial space for your business, there are many other factors that you must consider. With a lease, you will be locked into renting the space for a specified period of time with financial repercussions involved for moving out prior to the lease expiration. Likewise, by purchasing property, you will be committing yourself and your business to a long-term debt. Before deciding to lease or purchase commercial property, be sure you and your business are ready for such a financial commitment.

Your business location will also determine liability issues and the need for insurance. As you will discover, liability is a main concern when determining the type of business structure to choose. There are more detailed considerations for choosing a location for your business and significant ramifications of your choice based on your business entity. *This will be discussed in Chapter 9.*

Entrepreneurial Skills

The lure of starting a business and working independently is strong, but the reality is that entrepreneurship is not for everyone. An entrepreneur is a unique individual with certain characteristics. You should answer the fol-

lowing questions about yourself before considering starting a business:

- Do you have a strong desire to be your own boss?

- Do you want to be the master of your own financial
  destiny, no matter what happens?

- Do you have specialized and significant business
  abilities based on your experience and education
  that will help you in your business venture? What
  are they?

- Do you have the conceptual ability to see the big
  picture rather than just the parts?

- Do you have the business sense to make the right
  decisions for a business, and the courage to stick
  to your convictions?

- Does entrepreneurship run in your family?

- Do you persevere and have the ability to deal with
  adversity?

- Do you have the energy and time to sustain a
  business?

- Do you have the support of your family to pursue a
  business venture?

Of course, not every entrepreneur answers "yes" to all the
questions above, but too many negative answers may be a
sign that you do not have the right personality to pursue
a business of your own. Operating your own business can
be an exciting venture, thus many aspiring entrepreneurs

think more about the freedom and flexibility of working for themselves than about what the work actually involves. As an entrepreneur, you will have no boss telling you what to do and when to do it, but you will also not have the security of knowing that there is a management structure handling paperwork, human resources issues, payroll, and all of the other administrative issues involved in running a business.

Consider if you can work independently, multitask effectively, and interact with a range of different clients. Most importantly, do you have what it takes to pursue a goal and not give up when you face obstacles along the way? There will be many hurdles — some small and some not so small. Planning and preparation help make those obstacles surmountable and will contribute to more successes, but you will need the stamina and perseverance to deal with both. Starting a business is a major undertaking, and one that deserves serious consideration before making anything official or spending any money. Take the time to take stock of yourself and then decide whether you are ready for the next step.

Time Management

For any successful business owner, good time management skills are essential. Sometimes, it is hard for a person to have the self-discipline necessary to keep work schedules and meet deadlines. If you have decided to start a home-based business, the problem can be even more pronounced with distractions like the TV, stereo, Internet, family dog, or refrigerator.

Think of your new business as you would any other job. You have things to do and a given time period in which to do them, just as you would have if you were working for someone else. Creating a task planner is helpful to get your work organized. More than just a to-do list, the task planner allows you to list your responsibilities, due dates, and the blocks of time you can devote to each task. When creating your task planner, keep in mind any potential family responsibilities such as soccer games or school plays. Actually use your task planner, and check off the tasks completed as you accomplish them on a daily, weekly, and monthly basis.

Keep an updated calendar in front of you at all times. Your clients will be depending on you to make deadlines. Forgetting or not writing things down is not an excuse. Organize your work in files that indicate timelines with important project dates. If you are running a retail business, create a system with reminders about order dates or upcoming special events that might affect your business. For example, you may need to order a certain item several weeks before a holiday promotion to ensure it arrives on time. Mark these dates on your calendars and your files, both paper and electronic. Set up reminder notes in your files and on your computer system.

If you are struggling to get yourself organized and to manage your time effectively, consider taking a training course on time management. Community colleges often offer such courses as part of their continuing education program with affordable registration fees. Time management and self-discipline are crucial to completing all the tasks needed when planning, starting, and growing your business.

Choosing a Business

Many aspiring entrepreneurs have an idea for a business that they have always wanted to pursue. However, some just know that they want to start a business but are not sure what type. Perhaps you know what you are good at and have chosen a business; you have carved out your market niche. If not, you need to decide what type of business to undertake. The first step is to assess your skills, experiences, desires, and talents. Put your assessment in writing and review it objectively to determine what kind of business would work best — not only for you, but also for potential customers. It is similar to creating a résumé. List your areas of interest that could be expanded into a business. Home in on those areas in which you have the most knowledge and experience — especially in areas that you enjoy. That last point is crucial. If you have decided to start a business because you are unhappy in your job, make sure that your new venture will not end up with the same result. By closely examining your experience, skills, and interests, you should soon arrive at a business that works for your strengths and talents.

Once you have decided what your business will be, do some research to be sure there is a market for your product or service. Check out potential competitors, conduct some informal surveys of friends or acquaintances, and read through the daily business news to spot trends. Beware of starting a business simply because no one else has ever done it. There may be a reason that there are no other businesses doing what you want to do — perhaps there is not yet a market, or the conditions (particularly economic conditions) are not suited for your idea.

Test the waters first before putting too much time or effort into your business idea. If there seems to be a solid, potential market and — based on your self-assessment — you determined that you have the entrepreneurial skills as well as the experience and talent, then press on with your new business idea. Otherwise, take a few steps back and reassess. You may need to tweak your idea to fit a changing economy, or you may simply need to take it in a different direction.

Your business name

Carefully consider the name of your business before printing out hundreds of business cards and letterhead. Your name should be a reflection of your business goals and image — and should be available for your use.

A business name should be memorable and appropriate to the type of business. Select a business name based on how you want potential customers to view your business. Is it fun and light-hearted, or professional and conservative? Many entrepreneurs choose a simple business name that reflects their own name, such as Smith Enterprises. This is a simple name that customers will remember but that tells people absolutely nothing about the nature of your business. Granted, it has worked for many people, like Procter & Gamble (yes, there was a Mr. Procter and a Mr. Gamble), but it is best to select a name that tells potential clients a little about what type of business you are in and what type of business owner you are. Think about the company name Toys "R" Us. There is no doubt about what this company sells. Even something simple like John Smith, Consultant will convey a little more information to potential clients. Regardless of the name you choose, once you decide on the name, you will need to take the appropriate steps to register and protect it.

The most important thing to do when selecting a corporate name is to make sure that no other person or business entity currently has the same name. There are two operative factors going on here. First, using someone else's business name may impose on their trademark or service mark rights. This could result in legal problems. Second, the secretary of state's office will not register your corporation if its name is already being utilized. A trademark and a service mark are essentially the same, except that service mark refer to a service and trademarks refer to a product, brand, or symbol. In either case, it is advisable to search for existing trademarks and corporate names to determine whether your selected name is in use.

Trademark searches can be done professionally for between $300 and $1,200. Nevertheless, you can avoid these charges yourself by using the Internet. Search registered and pending trademarks at the U.S. Patent and Trademark Office (USPTO) Web site (**www.uspto.gov**) and use the Trademark Electronic Search System (TESS). Go to the New User Form Search, type in the name you want to use, and click "Search Term." Be certain that the "Field" term is on "Combined Word Mark." To make sure that your search is comprehensive, be certain to perform the following:

- Enter all phonetically similar names of your company because names that are phonetically similar can cause conflicts in trademark use. For example, if you want to name your company Netflicks, you should enter Netflix as well.

- Enter the singular and the plural of your company's proposed name.

- If your proposed name has more than one word, enter each word separately.

- Use "wild card" search terms, such as the asterisk (*) to broaden your search. For example, if you are searching for Netflicks, you can enter Netfli*, to search for similar names that began with the same six letters.

Be advised that trademark searches are not foolproof. Searches reveal only those names that are registered. There may be unregistered business names that are in use as well. They would be considered valid even if they may not have shown up in the USPTO database. Consequently, after searching there, you should search the Internet for the proposed name. This would probably reveal any current users of your proposed name. If you have reached this stage without discovering any conflicting trademarks or service marks, you should then search the secretary of state's records for existing corporate names. Most states offer free searches of existing corporate names, generally through their Office of the Secretary of State. *A listing of the states' Office of Secretary of State Web site is provided in Appendix A.*

If your name passes the previous tests, you may want to reserve it. This step is not absolutely necessary but is recommended as you move through the planning and development stages of your new business. Most states offer a reservation service where you file a short name reservation form with the secretary of state, but there is a fee for this service that will vary with each state. When you have finalized your name, make sure that you have an appropriate corporate suffix to make the public aware of your limited liability protection, if you have decided to incorporate your business. Include:

- Corporation or Corp.
- Incorporated or Inc.
- Limited or Ltd. In some states, this suffix can be confused with a "limited partnership" or "limited liability company."

Financial considerations

Examine your financial projections as well as your current situation to ensure that you have a solid foundation for launching and operating your business. Depending on the nature of your business and the economic conditions at the time you launch your venture, you may not make a profit for the first year — or even the first two years — of operation. You will need to have a plan for paying the bills while your business is getting off the ground. You might consider taking on a part-time job that will allow you to focus on your business in your off-time, or possibly even taking a personal loan from a friend or family member. The best plan is to have enough savings lined up to cover at least a year's expenses before starting your new business venture.

Your financial needs will vary depending on the type of business form you choose. For a sole proprietorship or even a limited liability company (LLC), you will probably be funding your business yourself or through small business loans, either through a financial institution or personal contacts. As will be discussed in the following chapters, however, funding becomes a little more complicated and possibly more available with the other legal structures. For example, corporations can sell stocks to raise money for the business.

Regardless of your chosen legal entity, calculate the amount you will need not only to sustain your business, but also yourself and any employees you might have. When considering your financial situation, use realistic projections based on information you will gather for your business and marketing plan, which is discussed later in this chapter. More detailed information about financial considerations for each type of business entity will be discussed in the chapters that follow.

Working with professionals

If you are planning to start your operation as a sole proprietorship, you may not need a lawyer immediately, as the paperwork is fairly simple and easy to understand. However, even with a simple structure, such as a sole proprietorship, it may be advisable to work with a financial professional who can help with bookkeeping and tax issues, such as an accountant, if that is not a particularly strong area for you.

You will need to consider several points, as you are choosing professionals who will help you with your new business, including: whether the accountant or lawyer has experience with small businesses; how much time you will need the professional to invest in your business; and, most importantly, whether you can afford to hire a professional at this stage of your business. Some help is available at no or low cost, such as small business counseling through your local community college. Selecting an accountant and lawyer can be more challenging and certainly more expensive.

If you want to hire a lawyer, you can ask friends and relatives for a recommendation. In addition, local bar associations have listings of qualified attorneys. Remember that costs vary, so you can expect to pay $100 an hour in rural areas and up to $350 an hour in metropolitan areas. As with most professionals, you pay for experience. Generally, you will not need a lawyer to prepare or file paperwork to launch a sole proprietorship. For forming corporations and LLCs, however, the process is much more complicated, so attorneys often charge a flat fee for forming corporations and LLCs, with total costs ranging from $500 to $2,000 for full-service incorporation packages.

Accountants' fees will vary widely, depending on the services you ask them to provide. If you are able to handle your day-to-day bookkeeping, including accounts payable and receivable, you may only need an accountant to manage your tax matters. Regardless of the type of professional services you may need, always do your homework on potential candidates. Ask business associates or your networking contacts for recommendations. Blindly choosing a professional from a phone book or Web site could result in unwanted consequences — unless you do your research on them first.

Small business counseling is available through a number of organizations, generally at no charge. Community colleges also offer seminars and courses for a reasonable cost, on topics from writing a business plan to maintaining records and filing your taxes. The Small Business Administration (SBA) is a federal organization with offices in every state. The SBA offers guidance and resources on its Web site, **www.sba.gov**. *A list of SBA state contacts is also provided in Appendix A.*

Business Plan

This book will examine the essential elements of your business plan and marketing plan, both of which must be developed prior to opening your doors for business. Although how to write a business plan is beyond the basic scope of this book, we will touch on it because it is an important first step in building your business.

In essence, a business plan is simply that — a plan for your business. To be successful, you need to know where your business is going and how it will get there. You will use a business plan as a guide to not only start your business, but also to expand it when necessary. Potential investors will also look at your business plan to get a sense of the solidity of your business idea and financial state. In fact, banks and other lenders will not even consider a loan proposal without a solid, well-written business plan that shows them your business has potential. The business plan must be accurate, succinct, and thoroughly researched.

Why create a business plan? Beside the fact that you will not be able to obtain financing from an outside source without one, organizing your thoughts and writing your business plan will help you take an objective, critical, detached, and unemotional look at your idea, your finances, and your plan for long-term growth.

On completion, the plan is a tool that — when used properly — helps you plan and manage your business properly and conveys to others that you have a sound blueprint for your business. Potential investors, in particular, want to see a solid business plan for reassurance. A well-planned and organized business plan that is used throughout the life of your business will increase your opportunity for success.

As the owner, you should actively participate in writing the business plan, although you may need to get some assistance with certain areas such as financial, marketing, or even the actual writing process. The plan should be used throughout each stage of the planning and operation of your business, specifically to:

- Make start-up decisions.

- Reassure lenders, investors, or backers that you have a solid plan for your business.

- Measure operational progress.

- Test planning assumptions.

- Adjust forecasts.

- Calculate ongoing capital and cash requirements.

- Set guidelines for good management.

Marketing Plan

In addition to the business plan, the marketing plan is an essential tool of the entrepreneurial business owner. It is the core of business reasoning. Especially in sales, the marketing plan enables the owner to develop consistent growth in sales by becoming knowledgeable about the market. A marketing plan simply answers questions such as:

- Who is the typical customer? (age, gender, family size, family income, location, buying patterns, reason to buy from you)

- Where is the market geographically? (county, state, national)

- What is the market in economic terms? (single family, average income, number of children)

- How large is the market?

- Who is the competition? This is important because no business exists in a vacuum. Get acquainted with the competition. Locate direct competitors, both locally and nationally, and in terms of product lines. List names, addresses, and products or services. Answer the following questions about your competitors:

    ➲ Who are the closest competitors?

➲ How are their products and services similar to yours?

➲ Do you have a unique "niche?" If so, describe it.

➲ How will your product or service be better or more saleable than theirs?

➲ Are their businesses growing? Staying the same? Declining? Why?

➲ What can you learn about the business from observing or talking to their current or ex-clients?

Remember, a solid marketing plan will keep you focused and on track. Your marketing plan should also include elements regarding sales and advertising.

Sales

There are many different methods of selling, so you should decide which one you are most comfortable with and want to employ for your business. The following are a few examples of the types of sales methods you can use in your business:

Direct sales: Made directly to the consumer. These types of sales are made by telephone, through cold calls or inbound calls to a customer service representative, or through a person-to-person method. For this method, careful research is recommended to determine if it is appropriate for your particular type of business and client profile. Retail businesses, for example, engage in direct sales.

Mail order: Generally most appropriate for retail business-es. Web-based businesses have proved to be successful at this type of sales plan.

Franchising: You may decide to buy into someone else's franchise or open up your own that sells rights to certain geographic areas or product lines to others. Research the legal, financial, and marketing ramifications for each one. The SBA publication *Evaluating Franchising Opportunities* is an excellent resource guide on this topic.

Advertising

As part of a marketing plan, each product or service will require its own advertising strategy. Before investing in any type of marketing or advertising program, review your product or service, your business goals, and your customer profile. You will want to be as effective as possible with your advertising dollars. In particular, you do not want to initiate an advertising campaign that will backfire or not deliver the message you intended regarding your business and products and services. Advertising's basic goals are to:

- Get sales orders or contracts.

- Promote special events, such as sales, business openings, or new products.

- Attract requests for estimates or a sales representative's call.

- Validate yourself before startup and to get customer feedback.

Advertising varies widely in its forms and its costs. You can plan a range of strategies, from distributing business cards for potential clients to creating a brochure to displaying ads in magazines or even on billboards. You could also reach potential clients with a telephone survey to inform them about your start-up plans and to develop a profile of your ideal client.

Once you have determined what types of advertising are important, you should consider the following:

- What media should you use?

- How much money do you want to spend on advertising?

- How can the advertising program be implemented?

- How can you track the effectiveness of the advertising?

Finally, address the following areas in choosing your advertising media:

- **Trading area:** Do you seek an industrial, national, or other market? Describe your market.

- **Customer type:** What are your potential customers' interests? Describe your customer.

- **Budget restrictions:** Although you may have to spend more in the beginning, it is recommended that advertising should not be more than 1 or 2 percent of sales.

- **Continuity of message:** Try to determine how the product or service you are offering — together with the customer profile and seasonal buying patterns — affect your choice of media and how often you advertise.

The key to the business and marketing plan is getting organized and putting everything down on paper. From the business plan to the advertising plan, it all starts as an idea. From there, the sky is the limit.

CASE STUDY: COUNTING YOUR COSTS

Ambrose Schulman
(Company name and contact information withheld on request)

Ambrose Schulman has practiced law for 40 years, and his experience includes expertise in government contracts, commercial law, and corporate law.

The cost of organization is important. That includes the use of a lawyer and any necessary filing fees required by government agencies. The simplest and least expensive business to organize is the sole proprietorship. Pick a name that does not duplicate or compete with another, obtain any required governmental permits, and you are in business. The flaw is that you have unlimited personal liability for the business's obligations, to the extent they are not covered by insurance. A better response to this problem is to form a corporation.

Today, the law in many states authorizes a single individual to form a corporation. If the traditional corporate form is used, counsel should be retained to prepare the corporate charter, bylaws, and minutes of the first or organizational meeting. Changes to the charter and bylaws should be prepared by counsel or another responsible person — usually the corporate secretary. Thereafter, minutes of the board of directors' regular and special meetings should be kept and maintained.

Ideally, we should form a team consisting of counsel, our accountant, and an insurance broker, and follow their advice as best we can, considering the amount of time and money available to us. You should consider having an accountant to maintain the books and records for the business. This should work to assure confidence among the principals (no cheating), government agencies (such as the IRS), and future investors. We should maintain the insurance required by law, such as workers' compensation, fire, casualty, and business interruption.

To find out how much it will cost to incorporate, check with your secretary of state — the office with whom corporations must register — and obtain the list of fees, or call them and see if they can send them to you or direct you to their site. The forms needed for a partnership are an agreement of partnership and, as noted, that can be a complicated document because it will involve issues such as division of labor, compensation, benefits, dissolution, and who makes the final decisions.

To save money when starting a new business, the basic rule is keep your overhead low, accept long hours, avoid (as practicable) using consultants to help you when you need them, maintain good but not lavish facilities, and offer incentives through stock options or bonuses for everyone in the business. The latter form of compensation made secretaries at Google and Microsoft millionaires. Plan your work, and work your plan. In short, select a business model and stick to it.

Chapter 2

Overview of Business Structures

This chapter will provide an overview of legal and financial considerations that can affect the choice of the form of business. The chapter provides a brief overview of each of the four major types of business entities, which will be discussed in detail in the following chapters.

Sole Proprietorships

A sole proprietorship is the easiest type of business to form. One-person business owners normally choose this type of business entity. Freelance writers, graphic artists, photographers, and consultants who work as independent contractors might elect to be sole proprietors based on the simplicity of ownership and little legal liability anticipated. Unlike with corporations, they may prefer not to deal with bureaucratic red tape and may want to start right away. The state and IRS will view you as a sole proprietor, meaning the IRS and the state will tax your individual earnings if you live in a state that collects taxes. Legally, your personal bank account and assets will theoretically be liable to collect debts incurred in the event of a lawsuit. There are few federal, state, or local laws governing the operation of sole proprietorship, unlike with corporations and, to a lesser extent, LLCs.

Partnerships

Partnerships are businesses where two or more individuals get together to run a business as co-owners and agree to share the profits and losses. Each partner agrees to contribute capital, property, hours, and expertise in exchange for monetary gain. If you join with only one partner and do not even sign a partnership agreement, you have still formed a general partnership. Although it is not legally necessary to draft a partnership agreement to form a partnership, most partners are conjoined by a written partnership agreement. Those who do not deem it necessary to draft a partnership may seal the deal with a handshake. These entities also may rely on oral agreements between or among its members. In any case, the business becomes a general partnership when there is more than one owner. Since disputes often arise between partners, it is advisable to have a written partnership agreement.

Limited Liability Companies (LLCs)

The limited liability company, or LLC, is a relatively new business structure that has been widely adopted. Small business owners embrace it because the states have legislated it to overcome the shortfalls of the other business entities, including corporations. In essence, it was conceived to preserve the pass-through taxation of sole proprietorships and partnerships where the profits are taxed on an individual's return — while, at the same time, limiting financial and legal liability to its members, as in a corporation. Thus, the members of an LLC pay taxes on the business's profits on their personal returns, but their personal accounts and assets are not subject to business debt or legal judgments.

Corporations

A corporation, like an LLC, is formed and governed by state law. What distinguishes a corporation from the other business entities is its existence as a separate, legal tax structure, apart from any and all of the owners or managers who control or run it; the corporation is a legal entity according to state and federal law. That signifies that the corporation can make contracts, have debt, and pay taxes completely separate from its owners. It is a legal entity apart from its owners and technically has a life of its own.

C and S corporations comprise the two types of corporations for tax purposes. The C corporation is the regular corporation formed for making profits and taxed under standard corporate income tax regulations. The "C" denotes Subchapter C of the Internal Revenue Code and distinguishes C corporations from S corporations, which are governed under the Subchapter S of the Internal Revenue Code. *Each will be discussed in detail in Chapter 6.*

Other Legal Entities

There are some business types that do not fit neatly into the four main categories discussed in this book. If you want to form a partnership with someone who will not have decision-making authority — often referred to as a silent partner — you will need to create a limited partnership. For partnerships with potential malpractice issues, such as a doctor's office, you will best be served by forming a registered limited liability partnership (RLLP).

Limited partnership

A limited partnership has two types of partners: A general partner, known as the managing partner, runs the business every day and also incurs its debts and claims. A limited partner, in contrast, only contributes to the business finan-cially. The limited partner does not get involved in the daily operations of the business and is not liable for the debts or judgments incurred by the business. A limited partner is similar in nature to a shareholder in a corporation, being a passive member of the company. They invest in the com-pany and hope that it grows so they can make a profit from their investment or make money from it when it sells.

Registered limited liability partnership (RLLP)

Registered limited liability partnerships, or RLLPs, may be formed in all 50 states as a special type of partnership, which is an alternative to an LLC. In some other states, RLLPs were created because state law did not yet recog-nize LLCs. In other states, RLLPs were invented to protect members in a company from the personal liability or mal-practice of other members in the company. This business structure is mainly geared for professionals with malprac-tice liability such as doctors or lawyers. Therefore, unless you are a professional seeking to form a company with other professionals, the RLLP is not the business structure you should choose.

Comparison Chart

The following comparison chart will help you visualize the basic differences in the four main business entity types:

Legal entity	Costs involved	Number of owners	Paperwork	Tax implications	Liability issues
Sole proprietorship	Local fees assessed for registering business; generally between $25 and $100	One	Local licenses and registrations; assumed name registration	Owner is responsible for all personal and business taxes	Owner is personally liable for all financial and legal transactions
Partnership	Local fees assessed for registering business; generally between $25 and $100	Two or more	Partnership agreement	Business income passes through to partners and is taxed at the individual level only	Partners are personally liable for all financial and legal transactions, including those of the other partners
LLC	Filing fees for articles of incorporation; generally between $100 and $800, depending on the state	One or more	Articles of organization; operating agreement	Business income passes through to owners and is taxed at the individual level only	Owners are protected from liability; company carries all liability regarding financial and legal transactions
Corporation	Varies with each state; can range from $100 to $500	One or more; must designate directors and officers	Articles of incorporation to be filed with state; quarterly and annual report requirements; annual meeting reports	Corporation is taxed as a legal entity; income earned from business is taxed at individual level	Owners are protected from liability; company carries all liability regarding financial and legal transactions

CASE STUDY: UPGRADING BUSINESS STRUCTURES

Dr. Jay Alperin Dentistry
Dr. Jay Alperin, DDS
2100 Lake Ida Road
Delray Beach, FL 33445
Phone: 561-272-2131
Web site: www.jayalperindds.com

I have been practicing dentistry for 34 years. I am a New York native, and I graduated from the State University of New York at Stony Brook with a B.A. in biology in 1969. I pursued my medical degree at the Medical College of Virginia and received my doctorate of dental surgery in 1973. I relocated to south Florida in 1973 and have been practicing dentistry there ever since.

When I launched my business, I financed through a local bank and actually began seeing profits in the second month of operation. To increase my visibility, I used my name as the name of my business.

As my dentistry practice grew and I brought on more employees, I decided I needed to incorporate my business. I now employ four people and operate my practice as a corporation. When planning this move to a new legal form of business, I decided to use a lawyer. I definitely recommend using one when choosing a business formation — they do a more professional job and can offer invaluable advice. As I was very busy with my practice and did not have time (or desire) to get involved with the paperwork, my lawyer was a tremendous help to me.

When searching for a lawyer to help with my incorporation process, I began networking. As it turned out, I knew my lawyer's boss. It was a good move, as I am happy with my choice of lawyers. He has saved me the aggravation of dealing with the eventual legalities involved. I have been quite fortunate in that I have not incurred any legal problems.

Chapter 3
Sole Proprietorships

The simplest form of business is the sole proprietorship. Even with its simplicity, though, a sole proprietorship requirexs a certain amount of preparation and paperwork. This chapter will provide the details of starting and operating a sole proprietorship.

In general, forming a sole proprietorship requires the least amount of paperwork of the four major types of business entities, and the type of paperwork you will need to submit depends on the local regulations of your city or county. If you have a home-based business, you will probably have to obtain a permit to operate out of your home. You will also need to secure a business license from your city or county. And, if you are operating under a name that is not the one listed on your birth certificate, you will have to submit an assumed name application to the state authority.

Financially, a sole proprietorship depends on the business owner providing the money needed to operate. You may decide to pursue a loan — through a financial institution with the help of the SBA or through a personal contact — but the ultimate financial responsibility lies with you as the individual business owner. As a sole proprietor, it is absolutely crucial that you have operating capital that will enable you to survive for the first few years without an income while your business grows. Some businesses do make money within the first year but most take at least that long to become established and to make more money than what is spent.

Tax Considerations

A sole proprietorship is not taxed as a separate business entity; rather, all earnings pass through to the business owner and are taxed at the individual level. The income produced by the business is considered to be the same as income earned by the business owner. As a sole proprietor, you will file your regular, individual tax forms but will also need to complete Schedule C (Form 1040), Profit or Loss from Business, as well as a Schedule SE, in which you calculate your self-employment tax.

The self-employment tax is essentially what you may have paid as an employee that will contribute to your social security earnings. However, when you worked for someone else, that company also paid their part of the social security tax. Now, as a self-employed sole proprietor, you are responsible for both parts, which will total just above 15 percent of your income. The good news is you will then be able to deduct half of that from your total income on your Form 1040 to reduce your overall tax liability.

Legal Implications

When you run your business as a sole proprietorship, any activities undertaken by the business are the same as activities in which you personally engage. As a sole proprietor, you are responsible for your business — financially and legally. In other words, if your business incurs debts, they become your personal debts. If a client sues your business for any reason, the client is really suing you — and for your personal assets.

That being said, unless your business is at substantial risk for financial or legal liability, the legal implications of operating as a sole proprietor are not substantial. If your business is service- oriented and you do not have clients coming to your office on a regular basis, there is little risk involved. However, if your business engages in activities that inherently carry potential liability risks — such as food preparation or a retail establishment — you will be susceptible personally to all of the potential financial and legal liability of your business operations. In these cases, a different legal form may work best for your business.

As a sole proprietor, you can also secure business insurance that will help protect you from the liability issues of your business. Costs and requirements for business insurance vary greatly with each state and with the nature and potential liability of your business. It is best to consult your insurance agent for advice on obtaining liability insurance for your business.

Operating a Sole Proprietorship

When operating your business as a sole proprietorship, you have complete control over how it is run. You are the sole business owner and are responsible for daily operations, marketing, financial issues, and all of the other aspects of running your own business. There are no partners or shareholders to whom you have to answer: only customers. As a sole proprietor, you are your business. While that can be a distinct advantage, it can also have its drawbacks.

Advantages and disadvantages

Although sole proprietorships are free from government regulation and simplicity in organization, they can be risky. Under this business entity, the business owner's personal and business assets are at risk, unlike corporations and LLCs. As a sole proprietor, your personal assets are the same as your business assets — as far as potential creditors and the legal system are concerned. Legal judgments that result in damages will be assessed against the business owner's personal assets, as well as the business's assets. This liability is the most dangerous aspect to this type of business entity. Granted, insurance coverage provides some protection for certain trades, but the premiums are so high that it may not be affordable. However, if you run a business like consulting from your home office and do not sell any food products or rarely have clients in your office, you run a very low risk in regard to liability issues.

Another drawback for the sole proprietor is the availability of business loans. For example, you may be a graphic artist who rents a home and wants to invest in a new program or computer to grow your business. Without collateral, it is extremely difficult to obtain money for a loan. Banks and other lenders are not likely to offer business loans to startup businesses because it is virtually impossible for an entrepreneur or small business owner to present a loan package to a bank officer with a cash flow sufficient enough to obtain the loan. Corporations, partnerships, and LLCs have better chances because these types typically have that substantial cash flow needed. Unlike corporations, which exist "in perpetuity," sole proprietorships only exist in the here and now. If you die, your business dies; your business does not "live" outside of yourself. Your assets and liabilities pass on to heirs, but the business itself no longer exists as you operated it. Your heirs may decide to continue the business, but they would have to essentially start it up again as a new business, in their name.

The sole proprietorship has its disadvantages, but it has its advantages as well. In a sole proprietorship, the owner has total control over the business. Unlike corporations, which are regulated, sole proprietorships have very little regulation. You can manage it whatever way you choose. Many business owners choose this business entity because of this freedom.

The simplicity of organization is also intrinsic to the sole proprietorship, unlike the other business entities, which have written agreements governing them. Again, there are no legal requirements other than keeping tax records. The business owner, who is beholden to no one, makes all decisions. No government agencies rule the operation of sole proprietorships, which is unlike corporations. Business licenses may be required, but they can be obtained easily by completing the appropriate paperwork and submitting it to a local authority, such as the city or county in which you will be doing business. If you are doing business under an assumed name (DBA), you may be required to file an affidavit with local regulators or publish a note in a local paper, to provide potential creditors with the true identity of the business owner in case a payment or legal issue arises. Finally, you may have to register with local, state, and federal tax bodies for an I.D. number if you do not use your social security number. This enables you to collect monies and pay taxes without exposing your personal social security number. The above are the only legal requirements for a sole proprietorship.

The sole proprietorship also offers tax advantages. Your losses and profits are personal expenses. Your losses are deductible from your profits, and the profits are only taxed once at the appropriate rate. This may be more advantageous than how partnerships are taxed, and how corporations are double taxed for the beginning stages of your company.

CASE STUDY: TAKING FLIGHT AS A SOLE PROPRIETOR

David Shapiro
Desert West Aviation
145 South Gene Autry Trail, Suite F
Palm Springs, CA 92262
Office Phone: 760-327-3636
Cell Phone: 818-326-1689
Web site: www.DesertWestAviation.com

I have always had an interest in flight, but with the responsibilities of raising two children, I put it on the back burner. As I approached my 50th birthday and with my children grown-up, it was time to realize my passion for flight that I had carried with me my whole life.

I had savings and investments from my previous printing business to finance it with. I then moved to Palm Springs, California, to begin the project that I call my second coming. This project is Desert West Aviation, a flight school with aircraft rentals. All the workers are independent contractors.

I consulted an attorney who is a personal friend, and he recommended starting as a sole proprietorship and incorporating later. I agreed to start as a sole proprietorship because it is easier, but I preferred hiring an attorney and getting professional advice. I have not had any legal problems yet, but I plan on incorporating later to protect myself against liability. The most difficult thing about getting started was finding office space in an airport.

I chose the business name based on geographical location and have registered it as a DBA (doing business as).

Chapter 4
Partnerships

E ssentially, a partnership is formed when two or more individuals get together to run a business as owners and agree to share in profits and losses. A partnership has many forms, but they all provide owners flexibility, relative simplicity, and ease of management, which are all similar to a sole proprietorship. Some partnerships (limited partnerships and limited liability partnerships) also offer a degree of liability protection, unlike a sole proprietorship. Partnerships are often the chosen business entity for retail and sales endeavors. Owners might want to pool their resources and split the profits. Bookstores, boutiques, DVD stores, thrift shops, and convenience stores are all examples of businesses that do well as general partnerships.

If a dispute between owners arises and they do not have a partnership agreement, state partnership laws preside, which is an umbrella-type legal regulation that applies for all sizes of partnerships. It states that profits and losses of the partnerships should be divided equally or, in some states, according to each partner's contribution. The laws also apply other rules for all partnerships that might not be appropriate for the size and nature of your business.

Therefore, it is advisable to draft a partnership agreement that delineates the issues that are vital to a business arrangement, such as splitting of profits and losses, withdrawals of monies, and the process for selling a partner's interest back to the partnership or externally, should a partner pass away or want to leave the partnership.

No fewer than two people comprise a general partnership, by definition, but there may be more than two partners. In fact, partnerships have no limit on the amount of partners they are allowed to have. Conversely, because they lack the management and organizational structure that LLCs and corporations have, partnerships with many partners may be difficult to operate. When there are more than two or three partners, it may be difficult to make decisions, and quarreling may occur. When this is the case in larger partnerships, managing partners may be designated by partnership agreements to make the business decisions. Yet, in smaller businesses, managing partners are rare because all partners are liable for debt and profit and want to have an active hand in managing the business.

Like sole proprietorships, owners in partnerships are liable for debts. For example, if you are running a graphic arts business and cannot make your payments on computer and printing equipment, your personal assets such as your car, house, and bank account will be subject to liens. In addition, if the business owes a creditor money, the general partner may be liable for the entire debt. The general partner may, though, sue his or her co-partners for their share of the debt.

General partnerships are extremely risky where personal liability is concerned. In a partnership, each general partner may bind the other partners to a contract or business deal, meaning that each partner is an agent of that partnership. When a partnership cannot fulfill its obligations under the terms of the deal or contract, is the other partners are personally liable for the amounts owed. In a sole proprietorship, only the one-person owner can make contracts, and in a corporation and LLC, the owners are not personally accountable for a business's debt, no matter who makes the contract.

In summary, to distinguish a partnership from other business entities for legal and tax purposes, consider the following factors:

- If and how the partner(s) carry out the provisions of the written partnership agreement.

- Relationship among its agents.

- Skills and productivity of the agents.

- Control each agent has over the allocated and distributed income.

Getting Started

As for the future of a partnership, if you expect to add more partners or owners, it would be better to form a corporation or LLC, which offers a more structured business entity to manage. If you are starting out as a sole proprietorship and you meet a couple of people who want to contribute to your business endeavor, keep a partnership in mind.

Besides the written partnership agreement — should you choose to do one — general partnerships are relatively simple and inexpensive to set up. They can even be sealed with a handshake or oral agreement, but this not recommended, as there would be no proof if a disagreement arose.

The following seven-step process will help you organize and create your partnership.

Step 1: Options for where to organize a partnership

Nevada and Delaware offer advantages of incorporating. However, the laws governing partnerships are more consistent and similar among all states. In fact, all states — with the exception of Louisiana — have adopted the Uniform Partnership Act of 1914, and approximately 35 states have adopted the 1994 and 1997 amendments to that act. The Uniform Partnership Act, a law covering the equitable distribution of assets in partnerships, is more widely adopted than the Uniform Limited Liability Company Act, which is only adopted by nine states. These acts provide uniform state laws regarding the distribution of assets, taxation, and other legal aspects of partnerships and LLCs.

The point of this discussion is that you should form your partnership in the state that offers the most convenience. The location choice does not limit where you can do business — you will be able to conduct business across the country. To be specific, if all the members of your partnership live and do business in one state, you should organize your partnership there. If the members of your partnership are spread out across the country, you should decide where the partnership's main office will be and organize there.

Partnerships, unlike LLCs and corporations, do not have to register or qualify to do business in another state. This freedom from registering to do business in another state is a significant advantage for a partnership. *General requirements and regulations involved in doing business in another state are discussed in Chapter 8.*

Step 2: Choosing your partnership's name

Once you agree to form a partnership, it becomes necessary to name it. You may use real names or a trade name, which is called "doing business as a fictitious name," or a DBA. Your partnership name is your legal name, while your trade name is your DBA name. For example, if your partners are named Jill Moe and Jane Lane, and you are both hairdressers, your legal name is Moe and Lane, while your DBA may be "The Hair Experience."

Before naming your partnership, you must be certain that both your legal name — which is your partnership name — and your DBA are available to use. You must make sure that your choice of name does not violate the trademark or service mark rights of other individuals or businesses. A trademark is any word, symbol, or use of both together used to express or name a product, service, or brand. A trademark does not have to be registered to benefit from legal protection. Trademark protection is intrinsic to the utilization of the mark in the marketplace. Suits arising from trademark infringement are common. *A more comprehensive discussion of searching for trademarks and service marks will take place later in Chapter 6.*

If your initial search of your partnership name does not result in a conflicting registered or unregistered trademark, you should then conduct an online search of existing company names with the secretary of state in the state where you want to organize. Remember, general partnerships do not need to register in states, so there will only be a few partnerships — those that registered voluntarily — listed in the secretary of state's database. Thus, this search is not very significant. On the other hand, limited partnerships must register with the state so that the secretary of state online search will be fruitful.

The name of your partnership must be indistinguishable from corporations and LLCs, in addition to other partnerships. The secretary of state will not accept a name that resembles another name, even if it is another business entity. For example, a secretary of state will not register Harvest Foods Inc. if there is another business named Harvest Foods LLC. Consult the secretary of state's Web site in your state to conduct free searches for company names in existence.

There are a few factors to remember when it comes to partnership names. If you are forming a limited partnership, your business name must normally contain an LP at the end. A general partnership does not have to reflect a "partnership" per se in its name, but it is suggested that it should so that your business entity is clear to potential customers and investors. The use of the word "partners" is desirable.

When using your business name, include only the legal suffix associated with your type of business entity. Otherwise, you may run into legal problems. For example, if you are a sole proprietor, you cannot name your company Howard Jones Inc. Similarly, if you are a general partnership, you may not call your company Jones and Smith LP. This practice is fraudulent and will leave you vulnerable to liability.

In addition, the following terms apply only to certain types of regulated businesses and are restricted from use in businesses' names by federal and state law, unless that business meets the legal standards for that term:

- Bank
- Thrift
- Trust or trustee
- Insurance
- Doctor
- Mortgage
- Investment and loan
- Cooperative
- Olympic or Olympiad

Step 3: Using an attorney

Once you have decided on a name, you must then decide if you want to hire an attorney to organize your partnership. There are pros and cons to each side. The greatest advantage to organizing the partnership yourself is saving money; you can also draft your own agreement. This will be discussed later in this chapter. Partnerships are much easier to form than LLCs and corporations. However, with any legal matter, cutting costs can hurt in the long run, especially if you do not have a partnership agreement.

Nevertheless, if you want to form a limited partnership where one partner incurs liability for the entire partnership; you have more than ten partners; or you have partners in multiple states, then hire an attorney, as these are especially complicated matters. An attorney can perform the following functions:

- Offer advice about alternatives and solutions to your business.

- Help with more complicated aspects of partnerships, like allocating profits, drafting the partnership agreement, and determining limited liability in limited partnerships.

- Foresee problems that may occur.

- Make sure that the business complies with federal and state securities laws when interests in the entity are sold to raise money if it is a corporation.

How can you find an attorney? You can ask friends and family for a recommendation, consult the local bar association, or ask for a referral. State bar associations also have a database of pre-screened attorneys. The hourly rate for business attorneys could vary from $100 to $350 per hour. Sometimes business attorneys charge a flat fee for forming partnerships and other business entities, ranging from $500 to $2,000. Always do your homework when considering an attorney to use in preparing your legal business documentation. Be sure the attorney has sufficient experience and expertise to accurately and efficiently help you with your specific business needs, and it is also a good idea to talk to previous clients for references.

Step 4: Assess ownership and make distributions

Partnership shares or interests will be allocated to the partners as part of the process of organizing your partnership. A partner's share of the ownership is called the percentage interest. You should determine each partner's percentage interest as a part of the ownership structure before writing the partnership agreement.

The owners of a partnership will have votes in proportion to their percentage interest in the partnership. For example, if a partner owns 75 percent of the company, he or she will have three-fourths of the votes in business decisions. Thus, even if that partner delegates managerial duties and operational functions to other managers in the company, his or her majority vote counts toward removing or appointing those same people. In summary, partners never assign their voting rights. They maintain their control and authority over the partnership.

How does capital contribution determine percentage ownership? Those who join a partnership give a capital contribution of assets for their stake in the business. Capital contributions can be in the form of cash, equipment, services rendered, promissory notes, or other obligations. In exchange for a capital contribution, he or she receives an interest in the company.

The percentage of ownership interest in the partnership depends on the amount of capital contributions made. For example, let us imagine three women want to get together to form a partnership. Aida gives $50,000 in cash, Beula gives $25,000 in computer equipment, and Cathy pledges

$25,000 in services to the partnership. In this case, the percentage interests are easy to figure out. Aida has 50 percent ownership, Beula has 25 percent, and Cathy retains the final 25 percent by virtue of their respective contributions.

The potential owners of a partnership will prefer to split the percentage ownership differently from their contributions. You can accomplish this in many different ways. One method is to change the value of the partner's contribution. In the above case, that would translate into changing the value of Beula's computer equipment to $35,000. She would then have a right to a greater percentage interest. Obviously, all partners must consent to these changes in valuations. Moreover, the valuations must be reasonable and realistic; the contribution of a desk cannot be valued at $15,000.

Another method by which contributions can be changed among partners is to assign a part of the partner's contribution as a loan. Thus, Aida's $50,000 contribution could be divided into a $25,000 loan and a $25,000 contribution. Together with Beula's $25,000 contribution and Cathy's $25,000 contribution, Aida would become a one-third owner with the obligation of paying back the loan at a later time. The loan does not earn Aida any more partnership interest.

It is advisable to determine each partner's capital contribution at the early stages of organizing your partnership. Each partner's capital contribution should be put down in writing in the partnership agreement. You should include in the partnership agreement a table that delineates the nature of each partner's capital contribution, the amount, and the percentage interest accrued by each partner. Be advised that the property contributed as capital contribution to the partnership becomes the property of that partnership instead of the individual owner. If that partner wants the property back, he or she must get the consent of the other partners. For the first example, a partnership agreement table might look like this:

	Capital Contribution	Amount	Ownership percentage
Aida	Cash	$50,000	50%
Beula	Computer equipment	$25,000	25%
Cathy	Services	$25,000	25%

You should also be concerned about distributive share, which is each partner's percentage share of the business's profits and losses. In most cases, the partner's distributive share is identical to his or her percentage of ownership. This is how partnerships and LLCs work. For example, say Bob owns 60 percent of a general partnership, and Maggie owns 40 percent. At the conclusion of the year, the partnership owns $10,000. They will split these profits according to their ownership percentage shares. Bob would receive $6,000, and Maggie would get $4,000 in distributive shares; if the partnership owed $10,000, Bob and Maggie would pay the same respective amounts. Ownership percentage share also determines how much money each party will get when the partnership is dissolved after the creditors are paid. Bob would get 60 percent, and Maggie would get 40 percent.

If you want to divide profits disproportionate to ownership shares, you deal in special allocation. Although legal, the

IRS is very strict with them to be sure that owners are not concealing income or apportioning losses to the owner in the highest tax bracket. The rules governing special allocation are extremely complex, so consult an attorney for this matter.

Step 5: Establish the management structure and select managers

The partners manage partnerships on an equal basis; this is built into the definition. This is called owner management. Nevertheless, general partnerships may occasionally designate partners as managing partners who have assigned to them certain duties. Normally, a managing partner is responsible for administrative functions, records, and supervision. Partnerships may select officers such as presidents and vice-presidents, but this is not common.

If you desire to select specific officers for your partnership, designate them in your partnership agreement and describe their duties. Although it is not absolutely necessary to designate each partner's duties in a partnership agreement, you may want to differentiate the managing partner's duties from the operating partner's duties, for example. Keep in mind that in a partnership, each partner is liable both financially and legally for the other partners' actions, and each may act as an agent for the partnership. Even nonparticipating partners can be liable for the actions of others. Therefore, stay in touch, stay involved, and stay informed.

Step 6: Write the partnership agreement

Now that you have decided on who will be a part of the partnership, the capital contributions of each, and how each partner's responsibilities will be split up, it is time to put it all down in writing to make it official. This document is called the partnership agreement.

The partnership agreement is the operational and founding document that establishes the rules of a partnership. The partnership agreement is to the partnership what the corporate bylaws are to a corporation. It rules on such issues as holding meetings, voting, quorums, distribution of profits, percentage of profits, and authority of partners. Partnership agreements are between five and 20 pages in length. Unlike the articles of incorporation — which are required for a corporation — they are not filed with the state. Your partnership agreement should include:

- The authority and responsibility of each partner and special responsibilities assigned to specific partners.

- Time and date of annual meetings, should the partnership decide to hold them.

- Procedures for expelling partners.

- Requirements for a quorum when partners vote.

- Procedures for written absentee ballots when voting is held at a meeting and a partner is absent.

- Special allocations, if any, of profits and losses.

- Total of each partner's capital contribution with its respective ownership percentage interest.

Once the partnership agreement is finalized to each partner's satisfaction, each partner should sign and date it. After that, the partnership agreement is the governing document of the partnership.

A partner ledger should be included in the partnership agreement as an appendix or as part of the body of the document. It is a written table drawing out the owners and ownership percentage interests of the partnership. The partner ledger is the same thing as a corporation's shareholder ledger and an LLC's membership ledger. If new partners are added to the partnership though the purchase of additional partnership interest (and accompanying capital contribution), the new owner is recorded on the list. The ledger should also show transfer of interest should a deceased partner pass his or her share of the partnership to someone else.

On the other hand, the partner ledger may not change if the partnership members remain the same. The partner ledger is a vital part of the partnership agreement. It is similar to the real estate deed. It shows evidence of partner's ownership, and it holds up in court if a dispute arises among partners regarding ownership interests. Partners should maintain a copy of an updated partner ledger at all times.

Step 7: Get an employer identification number

Because your partnership is considered a legal entity in the eyes of the government, you must obtain an employer identification number (EIN), also known as a federal tax identification number, according to federal law. You will also need this number to open a bank account. It is a simple procedure. Simply fill out IRS Form SS-4, Application for Employer Identification Number, or fill out the form online at **www.irs.gov**.

Tax Considerations

As for payment of taxes, a general partnership is similar to a sole proprietorship with its pass-through tax status. This IRS term simply means profits and losses for the business pass through to each individual owner's tax return that pays taxes on a personal return.

Partnership tax returns are not as simple as sole proprietorships; therefore, partnerships may need to hire an accountant. Although partnerships do not pay their own taxes like corporations, they must file an informational return annually: Form 1065, U.S. Partnership Return of Income. In addition, the partnership must turn over to each partner a record of the business's profits, losses, and deductions in Schedule K-1 (Form 1065), Partner's Share of Income, Credits, and Deductions; this form enables each individual partner to complete his or her individual tax return. Like LLC members, each partner is liable for taxes on profits, even if the profits were reinvested to grow the business instead of given to partners. This is technically known as allocated profits against distributed profits.

Take, for example, the following: Billy is an unincorporated used bookstore owner. He is the sole owner of the business and thus its sole proprietor. Annually, Billy files a

Schedule C (Form 1040), Profit or Loss From Business. He pays his individual income taxes on net profits. He also pays self-employment (social security and medicare) taxes that are calculated from Schedule C and computed on 1040 Form SE. Soon the business grows, and Billy takes in two partners. The three agree to share the workload, profits, and expenses. From that point on, Billy files IRS Form 1065, U.S. Return of Partnership Income, and gives his other two partners a 1065 K-1, Partner's Share of Income, Credits, and Deductions, which gives the correct figures for his partners to report on their individual tax return. As each partner is also active in the business, they also report their income on Form SE and pay self-employment tax on that amount.

Because a partnership has a life outside of its owners, things operate a bit differently than with a sole proprietorship. This separateness between the business and the owners results in what is known as "phantom income" to the partners — income that is taxed to a partner, even though he or she never receives it.

A partnership, like a sole proprietorship, is eligible for pass-through taxation. Therefore, all profits pass through the business and end up on the individual's tax return. Nevertheless, a partnership differs from a sole proprietorship in that the partner may never see the income received. The partnership agreement establishes how much of the money that the partnership earns is paid out to partners.

The concept of being taxed on money you do not receive is distasteful enough, but what can be more aggravating is having to come up with the money to pay the government each year. To avoid this situation, partners often adapt a procedure to ensure that the partners receive a minimum amount from the partnership to at least cover their taxes on this phantom income. A provision known as a distributions clause is often added to the partnership agreement that requires earnings to be allocated to the owners annually in a sufficient amount to cover taxes due on the profits earned by the partnership.

Legal Implications

Operating a partnership differs from corporations and LLCs insofar as they are created by the actions of their members, and not by the filing of paperwork with a government authority. In some cases, partnerships are simply formed by a verbal agreement to share profits in a business enterprise. Because of the lack of paperwork and informal structure, partnerships are more easily formed than LLCs or corporations.

Specifically, general partnerships do not have to register with the secretary of state's office as limited partnerships do. For example, you can register your general partnership in Delaware and California, but it is not required. Yet, these same states require registration of limited partnerships. Limited partnerships involve different tax structures and liability limits for the partner not involved in the management of the company.

When you register your partnership, you will be required to submit a filing fee. Registering the partnerships requires you to identify the members involved in the partnership, thereby leaving individual members exposed to an aggressive plaintiff wishing to sue the persons of the partnership. Therefore, it is not recommended to register a general partnership in any state. Remember, legally, you are not required to register your general partnership.

Advantages and Disadvantages

One advantage of a partnership is its ability to raise capital. For example, in a sole proprietorship, you are limited to your own resources, whereas in a partnership, you have the potential resources of as many partners as you choose to go into business with. Partners may use their credit line or bank accounts. When these resources are combined, there is a greater pool of capital than if you go into business for yourself. Still, financing with an established banking or lending institution is best obtained with a corporation.

Similar to a sole proprietorship, you may enjoy certain tax advantages that you would not enjoy under a corporation. The profits earned by a general partnership will pass through to owners without the double taxation that corporations have when they must distribute dividends to shareholders. Income derived from partnerships is taxed as personal income and taxed accordingly. Nevertheless, if a partner obtains a large income from the partnership, this can prove to be a disadvantage. The amount of taxes owed depends on the total income of each partner. As a whole, the partnership is not taxed, though.

The major disadvantage of a partnership is the possibility of clashes among members. Many partnerships have spawned legal disputes. This frequently occurs when there is no partnership agreement, and each partner's duties are not specifically outlined. Even still, consider how your partnership will be managed and by whom.

Another disadvantage to the partnership is the liability incurred by each partner for the debts of the company. This liability is even greater than in a sole proprietorship: In a sole proprietorship, you are responsible for the debts only you incur; in a general partnership, you are responsible not only for your debts, but for the other partners' debts, which may or may not be within your control. You can see how this can lead to potential conflict and dissolution of the partnership.

In a general partnership, not only are you subject to financial liability, but you are subject to liability regarding legal issues as well. You and your partners are bound by either a written or oral agreement to be liable for the actions of each other on behalf of the business. If one of your partners gets sued for not paying a debt, you must assume part of that debt. You can purchase general liability insurance to cover legal liability, which might be useful in the event of negligence from your business partner.

Similar to the sole proprietorship and unlike the corporation, the partnerships lack perpetuity. That means it exists only insofar as the partners run or manage it. It does not have a life or existence outside of itself; it dies when a partner dies. Broadly, a partner dies, a final accounting is done, and assets and liabilities are divided, unless otherwise specified in the partnership agreement.

Finally, because of the nature of its structure, partnerships do not have the same potential for raising capital as S corporations. Corporations obtain financing through public stock offerings; partnerships cannot do that. In addition, partnerships cannot offer certain benefits, like pension and profit sharing to their employees, as S corporations can.

Limited Partnerships

A limited partnership has one general or managing partner who is liable for the debts and judgments of the partnership and at least one limited partner who is not involved in the management of the business. This feature differentiates it from a corporation or LLC, where all members are covered by liability protection. Limited partners may not get involved in the management of the business, unless they wish to lose their liability protection. For this reason, few owners choose the limited partnership. If they want to invest money and run the company, they cannot have personal liability protection under the limited partnership. So, if you plan on investing in your company, being active in its operation, and wanting liability protection, this business is not for you; an LLC would be a better choice.

Limited partnerships are taxed in the same manner as general partnerships when it comes to income tax purposes — any income is reported on the individual's tax returns. Form 1065, U.S. Partnership Return of Income, is filed for informational purposes on behalf of the limited partnership, just like for the general partnership. Each partner gets a copy of Schedule K-1 (Form 1065), Partner's Share of Income, Credits, and Deductions, from the partnership where his or her profitable income is reported. This form is then attached to the individual's tax return. Limited partners do not have to pay self-employment taxes. Their share of the profit is not considered "earned income," even though they contributed financially to the operations of the business.

By definition, a limited partner does not participate in the management of the company. However, there have been legislative revisions that provide exceptions to the rule, particularly in regard to permitting a limited partner to participate in determining the partnership's structure, such as removing general partners, dissolving the partnership, revising the partnership agreement, or selling assets. But when all owners desire to participate directly in running the business, it is best to choose an LLC or a corporation. LLCs and corporations both provide owners who run the company with liability protection.

Despite its limitations, some companies still choose to be limited partnerships rather than LLCs, particularly if one of the partners does not want to be actively involved in the management of the business. An example of a typical limited partnership is an investment firm where investors feel that if general partners were liable for business debt — as they are in a limited partnership — they would be less likely to make bad business decisions. Though, in larger limited partnerships, the general partner can be an LLC or corporation where the personal assets are safe under the personal liability protection provided by those two entities.

The following example demonstrates how limited partnerships and corporations can work together. In 1980, before LLCs came into existence, a limited partnership named Calweb Holdings was formed as a real estate development company. Calweb Corporation has 20 limited partners and is Calweb Holdings' general partner. The limited partners invest cash to buy and improve the properties without managing power, while Calweb Corporation manages the property of Calweb Holdings for a fee. David and his son Jake own Calweb Corporation. Both the general partner, Calweb Corporation, and the limited partners of Calweb Holdings divide the profits of Calweb Holdings — that is, all of the partners of the limited partnership share in the income of the properties.

What we see here is that the general partner, Calweb Corporation, is a corporation. In bigger limited partnerships, especially if there is a possibility of large liability, this is a common method to curtail the personal liability of the general partner. For this example, real estate debts can be huge, and the possible liabilities connected with the remodeling and sale of properties — contractor liability claims, vacant properties, and purchasers reneging — are also quite large, and court costs can be astronomical. It was wise for David and Jake to form a corporation to protect themselves from this potential liability. Today, David and Jake would most likely choose a one-man-managed LLC to hold and develop the real estate, so he and his investors would be protected from liability.

Forming a limited partnership is as easy as paying a fee and filing papers (frequently called a "certificate of limited partnership") with the state. These papers are similar to the articles filed on behalf of LLCs and corporations, and incorporate data about the general and limited partners. Costs are about the same as those for LLCs and corporations.

As we have touched on in previous chapters, the limited partnership does not carry much liability protection. The managing partner — and there might be more than one — remains personally liable for debt. The LLC provides limited liability protection for the unincorporated business entity — those who do not wish to form a corporation. It provides inexpensive liability insurance protection over and above the expensive commercial insurance policies available.

Registered Limited Liability Partnerships (RLLPs)

Registered limited liability partnerships (RLLPs) may be formed in all 50 states as a special type of partnership and an alternative to an LLC. In California, for example, RLLPs were created because state law did not yet recognize LLCs. In other states, RLLPs were invented to protect members in a company from the personal liability or malpractice of other members in the company. This business structure is mainly geared for professions with high malpractice liability, such as doctors or lawyers. Therefore, unless you are a professional seeking to form a company with other professionals, the RLLP is not the business structure you should choose.

An RLLP, as its name suggests, is a partnership where each member is liable for his or her own actions but not for those of other members of the firm. RLLP state statutes also offer the professionals personal liability protection from other tort liabilities — such as doctors' personal injury lawsuits — of the RLLP in addition to business debt. You can see that RLLPs are perfect for doctor offices and law firms because they offer personal liability protection from cases in which clients can sue members. These cases can cost millions if you are a doctor or a lawyer and you want to protect yourself.

What are the requirements for an RLLP? It is necessary to have at least two partners for an RLLP. According to state statute, all partners must be licensed in their respective field. As we have mentioned, individuals who work in the medical, legal, or accounting field who have a professional client relationship would be eligible to work in an RLLP; veterinarians, engineers, and acupuncturists may also be allowed to form RLLPs in some states. Other states are more restrictive in the licensed professionals who are permitted to form RLLPs, since they protect personal assets in the case of malpractice, for example. It is common for states to allow the same professionals who form corporations to form RLLPs. Check with your state's LLC filing office to determine which professionals are permitted to form RLLPs in your state.

RLLP members enjoy a privilege not offered to other partnerships. Although owners are personally liable for malpractice suits resulting from their individual actions, they are not subject to monetary damages resulting from malpractice suits from other members or owners of their partnership. Moreover, in more than half of the states, owners are not responsible for any other type of liability incurred by other members of the firm, whether it is a contract dispute, tort, or malpractice. This is called the "full shield" limited liability protection of the RLLPs.

RLLPs, like partnerships and LLCs, are taxed as pass-through tax structures. That is, your profits are added to your personal individual tax return. The RLLP, unlike a corporation, is not taxed in and of itself because it does not have an existence outside of its owners. The monies are normally available as profit at the end of each year because most RLLPs are service-oriented and do not have to deduct monies for inventory like other retail-oriented businesses.

For all intents and purposes, RLLPs are like LLCs. Both provide pass-through taxation and limited personal liability. What differentiates the two is that RLLPs provide members liability protection from their partners' malpractice, while LLCs do not. For the average LLC owner, this is not a problem; legal liability arises from contract disputes, accidents on the ground, and complaints about the product — not as an act of malpractice between, for example, an attorney and a client. The latter is an extenuating circumstance where members should protect themselves in an RLLP.

A professional in any company — a partnership, LLC, RLLP, or corporation — is personally responsible under state law for malpractice. Yet, RLLP statutes provide protection form liability for other members' malpractice within your company. Under state RLLP law, you are not personally liable for the monies due to your partner arising out of malpractice suits. This type of protection is not regularly offered by state LLC statute.

Another difference between LLCs and RLLPs is the manner of distribution of its profits. Many professional organizations wish to give freely all net profits of the business, and RLLPs enable you to do that. This is possible because there is no inventory to deduct or other expenses to interfere with, making the business solvent (able to pay its bills on time). When these situations do arise, LLC laws dictate that distributions cannot be made to owners until all company bills are paid — that is, distribution cannot be made if doing so would make the firm insolvent; a RLLP is not governed by these limits. As an aside, most LLCs do not distribute each and every penny of profit to its owners, so these restrictions are often irrelevant.

The laws governing the formation of RLLPs and LLCs for professionals vary from state to state. Many states permit professionals to organize an LLC or RLLP. Some states do not allow lawyers, doctors, accountants, and engineers to create LLCs and only allow them to form RLLPs or professional corporations. In California, licensed professionals are not allowed to organize LLCs, and only lawyers, accountants, and architects can join RLLPs. So, if you are a professional who does not fall in one of these categories and want to limit your liability, you must form a professional corporation.

CASE STUDY: CHALLENGES FACED AND LESSONS LEARNED

Brenda Marchese
ChessMar Enterprises
chessmarent@rogers.com
Web site: www.handbaggems.com

I chose to become a sole proprietor because there is only myself and my daughter in business. We work from home, and the current nature of our business does not require having inventory in our home. We realized it would take time to make the income we want, so based on advice from various sources, this was the best step. Should we grow, we will consider the next step to become a corporation.

We learned these lessons while planning our business:

- **Decide what to do:** Am I going to sell product or a service?

- **Have more than one idea:** Have a backup plan should your business not work out. We came up with numerous ideas because we probably would not make money right away.

- **Plan to ask for help:** I did not assume I knew everything about running my own business. Although I have more than 35 years' experience within a manufacturing operation and had a fair idea of how it would work, I do not know all of it, and nor are my strengths in every field.

- **Increase your network:** While working, I had a very limited network, and I knew if I was to be successful, that network would have to expand — through sources such as local groups (through the counseling program my company paid for), Facebook, Twitter, LinkedIn, small business groups within my area, Entrepreneur Connect, *Shepreneur* magazine, and workshops to name a few.

- **Prepare to do some research:** Use the library, a mentor, someone else who is successful in his or her business, or the Internet. The Internet is chock-full of information about running a small business.

- **Attend any workshops:** I could learn more and from many different people at these workshops. There are a lot of free workshops (at least in my area) and especially check the government sites. I have attended a few workshops on how to run the business within government requirements (taxation, importing, etc.).

- **Be realistic:** I was realistic about my expenses, my plans, goals, my support, and, most importantly, my emotions, and was prepared to deal with that. This is not a fairy tale — the minute you open your doors, you will not make your first million.

- **Have a plan on how the business will work:** In your head is OK, but written down puts a timeline on the goal. I did not write one down, and I should have because it has taken me longer than I wanted. I do intend to create a formal business plan just for myself with the steps and timeline required.

- **Determine your schedule:** I decided that I would work just as I had before: getting up, showering, dressing, and working my time throughout the day. In some cases, this has also meant on the weekends or at night. This allows me to be focused on maintaining my goals for that day.

These were some of my challenges:

For me, deciding what to do was the most difficult. What do I do, what can I do, will I have something to offer that someone would be willing to pay for? You need lots of ideas with a backup plan ready to go if the first idea fizzles.

Deciding what investments to make to secure the tools needed to run the business was another one. You have to be a savvy consumer because there are numerous people who will sell their mother to you with one hand and after you have paid, take her back before you know it. Be wary of the phrase, "Don't you want to invest in your business to make it a success?" Yes, you do, but remember, until you get a return on your investment, it is still an expense. You need to ensure you receive value for your expense. For example, I purchased a Web site development software from a U.S. company, where if I had been more aware and done my research, I could have done this locally and received the same type of package, and probably for less money (especially on the exchange — lesson learned).

I also had problems with researching how to run a small business. There is an enormous amount of information from various sources you need to plough through to get a basic understanding on how and if can you even run a small business. It can at times be so overwhelming that you start to question your decision.

I also had to taking a good, long look at myself, analyzing my strengths and weaknesses. That is the most challenging aspect because we have to be honest with ourselves. Too often, people have an inflated sense of their own worth and tend to think they know it all, jump in without research, education, or help, and then when they fail, wonder why, On the other side of the coin, be careful not to be harshly critical of yourself. You need to think outside the box, research, educate, ask for help, and at least try.

Not having a written business plan either informally or formally has delayed the deployment of my business (and my income) later than I wanted. At the time of this writing, it is not critical, but I now have to be cautious.

Finally, a challenge for me was dealing with the emotions. One day you can be at the top of the world — for me, it was the day my Web site was finally published. The next day, you are living in abject terror and fear that you will not sell a thing, and you will run out of money and be on the street before you know it. I have had many a sleepless night since I lost my "regular" paycheck.

My advice to others, particularly in these areas, is:

- **Self-discipline:** Research, learn, educate yourself, ask others, and plan. By doing that, you can make appropriate decisions for the next steps.

- **Choosing a legal form:** If you have a small or home-based business, I would recommend a sole proprietorship.

- **Using professionals:** Use lawyers if you are incorporating, and accountants, especially when trying to do your taxes.

- **Time management:** Your time is your own, whether you choose to work that day and for how long. If you want your business to work, you will have to put time into it. It will not happen unless you do that. The challenge is how much is put to the business and how much to your family and leisure. Ultimately, it is your decision based on your goals.

Chapter 5
LLCs

A limited liability company (LLC) is a relatively new form of business that provides a number of benefits to the small business owner with few disadvantages. LLCs are also relatively inexpensive and simple to establish. A LLC can be formed with only one owner, or it can have multiple owners. Owners of LLCs are referred to as members. If you have more than one member, it is a good idea to draft an operating agreement. Such an agreement is not required but will prove useful in determining how your business will be run and which members will be responsible for which areas of operation. To establish your LLC as a legal entity, you will need to file articles of organization with your state, usually with the secretary of state's office. Articles of organization list the basic information about the business, such as who the owners are, where the business will be located, and how the LLC will be managed. If you already have an operating agreement written, it will be easier to provide the information necessary for the articles of incorporation. Filing fees for LLCs are generally reasonable; on average, they will not be more than $100. Some states do charge an annual tax on the LLC, recognizing it as a separate entity. *Refer to the state listings in the Appendix for the Web site providing the information relative to your state.*

Organizing an LLC alone may be scary at first. Yet, it is just a string of easy tasks. As always, you have the option of using an attorney for peace of mind and security. We will first examine what makes up an LLC. Then we will take you through the 10 steps in organizing one. The person or entity that organizes an LLC is known as the LLC organizer; this person signs and files its articles of organization or certificate of organization with the secretary of state's office or other governmental agency. An organizer is essential because a new LLC is without managers and owners. The organizer is similar to an incorporator of a corporation — the founding individual. The organizer may also be an owner or manager of the LLC but is not necessarily so. As the LLC's first representative, the organizer gives birth (in essence) to the LLC with his or her execution and submission of the articles of organization. With the execution of the articles of organization, the organizer subscribes to the honesty of the articles. Yet, the organizer does not undertake any real liability or responsibility. An attorney may also be the organizer of the LLC on behalf of a client. After the organizer finishes the organization of the LLC, he or she turns over the reins of the LLC to its owners.

After the organizer creates the LLC, individuals then become members by buying LLC membership interests — initial capital contributions. Upon joining an LLC, members sign an operating agreement. The LLC operating agreement delineates the operating guidelines of an LLC and supervises the responsibilities and rights of its members. Members or managers are voted in or are appointed to the LLC to manage the company. Member-managed LLCs operate like a partnership — all members participate in management. In manager-managed LLCs, all members do not necessarily participate in the management of the LLC. In manager-managed LLCs, the members appoint the managers who are responsible for the daily operations and decision-making of the LLC. This structure is equivalent to the board of directors of a corporation.

An LLC's managers do not necessarily have to be members. The operating agreement, in addition to spelling out management processes, dictates the relationship between managers and members and how they are appointed. The managers can act broadly and have the power to do the following:

- Write stock
- Enact mergers and acquisitions
- Obtain loans
- Develop employee incentive plans
- Enact purchases of real estate
- Supervise the company daily
- Terminate and hire workers
- Execute and approve contracts
- Handle customers and suppliers
- Keep the limited liability records

The management structures of the LLCs are restricted only by the creativity of the organizers. They can be run like sole proprietorships or partnerships. LLCs are so flexible that they can even be structured after the paradigm of a corporation; for example, an LLC can form a board of directors and have a CEO and president. Some

LLCs are so small that they only have a few members and managers. Commonly, LLCs have one member and one manager. The possibilities for management structure are endless. Yet, they first must be outlined in the operating agreement to take effect.

Getting Started

A LLC must file the articles of organization and pay the appropriate filing fees to the secretary of state office. Some states have corporation offices with different names, yet they all operate in the same manner. *A listing of each state's secretary of state office can be found in the Appendix.* You must submit periodic reports to the secretary of state's office, as well. If the LLC fails to pay its taxes, the secretary of state may withdraw the LLC's good-standing status. Operating agreements do not get filed with the secretary of state, but the secretary of state maintains records for businesses and is often referred to by creditors seeking to collect a debt. Now that we have given a brief overview of the features of an LLC and how it may operate, let us discuss the specific steps one must take to form one.

Step 1: Choose where to organize

These are several factors to consider when organizing a LLC:

- The state or states in which you conduct business
- The cost of filing fees for LLCs
- The cost of annual filing fees and annual reporting requisites

- The privacy rights offered by the state and other advantages

Normally, if you have a small business and only do business within one state, you should organize in the state in which you do business. LLC law is more consistent throughout the country, especially when it comes to taxation, so it is best to organize in your home state when forming an LLC.

But what if the LLC does business in more than one state? You may be required to register in all states where you do business, regardless of where you initially filed your articles of organization. State laws require that out-of-state LLCs — known as foreign LLCs — register and pay fees in the state where they are conducting business as a guest. This process is known as qualification. Not every LLC in the country abides by the foreign LLC requirement. Registration fees can be expensive — as high as $1,000 in California. Some states have specific requirements for what constitutes doing business in a state. Other states like California consider a single transaction as doing business in a state. Check the state's statutes if you are uncertain whether you must register. *You can do this through the state's Web site, provided in a list in the Appendix.*

States require this registration for qualification to raise money for the state and to protect consumers from unsavory business practices. If the name and address is registered with the specific secretary of state office, the business is visible and can be located by creditors and potential litigants.

Step 2: Decide on the name for your LLC

Once you have decided where to organize your business, you must decide on a name. Remember, you may use a trade name, but you must file a DBA (doing business as) form with your county clerk for using a fictitious name.

The most important thing to know when selecting an LLC name is to make sure that no other person or business entity currently has the same name. As with any type of business form, you will want to conduct a thorough search to determine whether your chosen business name is available. *Use the state Web sites listed in the Appendix to search your secretary of state's database of registered business names.* You will also want to search the U.S. Patent and Trademark Office Web site (**www.uspto.gov**) for registered trademark names.

When you have finalized your name, make sure that you have an appropriate LLC suffix to make the public aware of your limited liability protection. Include:

- Limited Liability Company or Limited Liability Co.
- LLC
- Limited and Ltd. (In some states, this suffix can be confused with a limited partnership or limited liability company)

Step 3: Registering your agent

A person or entity who is responsible and bound to receive legal papers on behalf of an LLC is a registered agent. The articles of organization designate the registered agent, but this agent can normally be changed upon the submission of a notice with the secretary of state. The registered agent acts in a special role. Because an LLC is not a physical human being, the entity would not be able to receive legal papers. The registered agent can be assigned with a simple statement, such as:

> The name and address in the State of California of this LLC's initial agent for service of process is Jane John, 420 S. Side, Los Angeles, CA 91306.

Registered agents may also be referred to as an agent for service of process or local agent, pending on your state. You can serve as agent, as can your family member, a corporate officer, an attorney, or a company that handles corporation and business services. Also, be aware that the registered agent's name is a public record. If you desire privacy, hire a professional. The agent must have a physical address in the state where the LLC is organized. Therefore, if your LLC does not do business in the state where you organized, it is necessary to hire a registered agent in that state. Take into account this additional cost when organizing out of state. Registered agents can cost from $50 to $150 a year. Business Filings Inc. (**www.bizfilings.com**) lists the services of registered agents in all states.

Registered agents can also be helpful in answering questions about filing fees, laws, statutes, and other information about the state you are filing in. They have an excellent rapport with the secretary of state and understand procedures. You may request sample articles of organization or ask them for recommendations for other sample corporate documents you may need. You should hire your registered agent either before or concurrently with the filing of your articles of organization to ensure that he or she receives the correspondence from the secretary of state.

Hiring a professional or an attorney for this function has its benefits. An attorney normally has a stable address and will understand the nature of the papers that your LLC has been served. In addition to legal papers, the agent will receive tax forms, annual LLC report forms, and similar official mail.

Step 4: Decide to organize yourself or use an attorney

At this point in the game, you should decide whether you want to organize your LLC yourself, hire an attorney, or hire a discount LLC service. The greatest advantage of organizing yourself is the money you save — although sometimes cutting costs now may cost you later in the long run.

You may want to hire a discount LLC organization service. Prices vary from $200 to $300, depending on the company you hire. They are normally competent and offer the following services:

- Submitting of articles of organization with the official state agency
- Drafting of a boilerplate operating agreement
- Minutes of first meeting of the LLC members

The following services are excluded, and you must do them on your own:

- Writing and editing an operating agreement
- Looking at and editing minutes for organizational meeting of members
- Holding members' organizational meeting
- Writing units or membership interests
- Complying with state and federal securities laws
- Submitting initial and periodic LLC reports

Nonetheless, discount LLC organizations offer quality services at a reasonable price. They cut through the red tape of bureaucratic offices and offer prompt and reliable service. Be aware, though, that the boilerplate operating agreement and blank minutes for organizational meeting that they provide can often be confusing to the novice organizer. Business Filings Inc. can offer comprehensive services ranging from $75 to $295 for the organization of your LLC, should you decide to go with a discount LLC organization service.

Your last option is to hire an experienced business attorney to organize your LLC. He or she can do the following:

- Offer ideas and solutions to your business problems

- Help in preparing the operating agreement and manager-managed LLCs

- Foresee problems before they occur

- Draft an operating agreement and minutes of the organizational meeting

- Make sure you are in compliance with state and federal securities laws when LLC ownership is sold or transferred

You can find attorneys through recommendations of friends or through your local bar association. The hourly rate for an attorney varies from $100 to $350 per hour, depending on experience and location. A flat fee of $500 to $2,000 typically covers the expense of organizing your LLC.

Step 5: The LLC ownership

As part of its organization, your LLC will underwrite ownership shares or units to its members. This is known as the member's percentage interest. For example, if an LLC underwrites 100 shares and issues 40 shares to one member, that member's percentage interest is 40 percent. Select your LLC ownership structure early in the organization process, preferably before submitting your articles of organization, so that the information will be spelled out clearly for all concerned prior to making your LLC a legal entity.

The members of the LLC vote in proportion to their percentage shares. For example, if the owner has a 40 percent interest, he or she votes 40 shares. Therefore, majority rules in LLC ownership. Even if managers are appointed and are not owners, owners have the voting power to hire and fire them by virtue of their ownership interest. Thus, members never delegate their voting power and have ultimate control over the LLC.

Initially, many states required LLCs to have two or more members. This led to a situation where owners would issue a 1 percent ownership right to a spouse or family member and keep 99 percent ownership, thus avoiding the single-member exemption. Now, all states except Massachusetts allow single-member LLCs. Today, there is no maximum limit on how many members may be in an LLC, but it is normally recommended to keep it where it will be easily managed.

Each member who joins a LLC should sign an investment representation letter. This document provides protection to the entity because in it, the member attests to his or her qualifications and experience. He or she also makes it known what his or her investment objectives are to ensure compliance with state and federal security laws.

Owners who wish to join an LLC issue a capital contribution in exchange for an interest in the business. This may be in the form of cash, property, services rendered, promissory notes, or other obligations. As a general rule of thumb, the amount of capital contribution made to the LLC translates into his or her ownership percentage. Sometimes, though, owners may want to divide ownership differently from their contributions. This can be done in different ways. One method is to alter the value of the contribution being made. Note also, that the value of the property must be rooted in reality. One cannot value a computer at $100,000. Members' capital contributions should be established at the planning stages or organization of your LLC and should be set forth in writing in the operating agreement.

Step 6: Draft the articles of organization

The LLC is born with the drafting and submission of the articles of organization. Normally, the articles of incorporation consist of one page and contain the following:

- LLC's name
- Agent for service of process's name and address
- LLC's purpose
- Names of initial members or managers (optional)
- Duration of the LLC (optional)

As a rule of thumb, do not appoint initial members or managers in your articles of organization unless it is asked for. States differ on this requirement. For example, in California, a listing is optional; in Nevada, it is necessary. You can elect members and managers for your LLC once the articles are submitted. The danger of including members' and managers' names in the articles of organization is that they are exposed to the public because the articles of organization is a public document.

Almost all of the secretary of state's Web sites have sample articles of organization. You should always use these samples when you file your articles of organization. These can be found at **www.learnaboutlaw.com**.

Step 7: Assemble your LLC kit and seal (optional)

An LLC kid contains a three-ring, loose-leaf binder where you keep your LLC records, such as the articles of organization, operating agreement, minutes of meeting, tax filings, and other important documents. The kit generally costs between $50 and $100. More expensive, leather-bound kits cost more. They contain the following:

- Sample operating agreement and minutes of meeting
- Blank stock certificates
- Seal

- Blank member ledger and transfer ledger
- Disc containing LLC forms

These kits are not legally necessary. If you do want the kit, you can purchase one in any office supply store for a reasonable price. The kit is useful to keep important documents that must be maintained securely in a safe place. The operating agreement, in particular, establishes the internal operating rules of an LLC and so should be kept in the kit. LLC kits contain models of the operating rules that might also be helpful to you. The LLC kit should also contain a seal that can embosses documents with your company's seal. The seal includes the name of your LLC, date of organization, and state of organization. The seal is impressed upon official documents like minutes and shows approval by the LLC.

Stock certificates are also included in LLC kits. Although they are usually not used by LLCs, some attorneys do recommend them for LLCs as a record of ownership. They may avoid disagreements over ownership issues in the future.

A membership ledger lists the owners of an LLC. It also indicates the percentage of interest held. When new members are added through the purchase of interests, the list is updated. Transfers of interest must also be recorded, such as when a member dies and leaves his share to a beneficiary. This membership ledger is extremely important, as it is similar to a deed for a property. The ledger provides the primary source of evidence of ownership and information that is significant in any legal situation, and must be meticulously maintained. LLC members should always receive updated versions of the membership ledger when it changes.

Step 8: Determine the management structure and select managers

Now that you have filed your articles of organization, your next task in organizing your LLC is to decide if you want your LLC to be member-managed or manager-managed. Nothing is set in stone, as you can always change your mind. For example, a member-managed LLC can become a manager-managed LLC with a member vote and an up-dated operating agreement.

As previously discussed, member-managed and manager-managed are the two types of management structures for LLCs. Owners manage member-managed, similar to how a partnership operates. This is the structure of choice for smaller LLCs because it is a simpler mode of organization; owners manage the business, and no vote is required of its members. Single-member LLCs are almost always member-managed LLCs. Appointed managers, who are not necessarily members, run manager-managed LLCs. This type of LLC is structured similarly to a limited partnership or a corporation. This structure is more complex because it requires voting and rules for appointments. Larger LLCs generally choose this type of management structure.

If you choose a manager-managed structure for your LLC, the owners must first reach consent on how many managers will run the LLC. One manager is acceptable for a small company, but larger companies normally have three managers where they benefit from the input of more than one person. In addition, a three-manager LLC prevents a single manager from acting out of self-interest. Conflicts of interest should always be avoided. For example, a member should not vote on the LLC's purchase of real property owned by that member because it would present a conflict of interest. Also, remember that an odd-numbered number of managers is preferable to an even number of managers to avoid deadlocks when making decisions.

After you choose your LLC's management structure and the number of managers you want, select the appropriate provisions for your operating agreement. If it is to be manager-managed, name the managers you have chosen. Remember, managers may or may not be members of the LLC. These managers serve the LLC on behalf of its members. An operating agreement, which will be discussed in the next section, should always contain provisions for how members can oust a manager if problems are arising. Members are entitled to vote on this action and should be provided with ample notice beforehand of the vote's scheduled date. Also, managers should not be appointed for an indefinite period of time, to allow for accountability.

On this note, it is interesting to note that LLC managers can be held liable for their actions on behalf of the LLC. Courts, though, are liberal when it comes to the prosecution recognizing the competitive nature of the business world. They abide by the business-judgment rule: It states, in essence, that courts will not look at managers' business decisions or hold managers accountable for errors in judgment, so long as they were:

- Independent and did not have a vested interest in the decision
- Acting in good faith
- Conscientious in learning about the facts

Step 9: Creating your operating agreement

The operating agreement of an LLC governs the internal affairs of the business. It governs such events as voting, holding meetings, quorums, elections, and the authority of members and managers. The document is five to 20 pages long. If you get the LLC kit, it should contain a sample that is suitable for your state. Operating agreements are not public documents; they are not filed with the secretary of state. They should be kept confidential and stored in your LLC binder or a loose-leaf binder.

You should draft the agreement carefully, and make sure you and the other members of the LLC thoroughly understand the provisions. You should sign it only after you are satisfied that you and others completely agree and comprehend what it sets forth. Never sign it without examining it closely. Operating agreements are essential. Although not legally required in all states, it is smart to have one. The first reason is obvious: Oral agreements can lead to disputes if there are varying versions of what was actually said. You are protected if you get all the rules and procedures down in writing to cement understanding among members and, if applicable, managers. When your LLC members do not prepare an operating agreement, your LLC will be supervised by the state default rules. State statutes establish these rules. For example, the default rules might state that an owner with a minimum of 10 percent ownership interest has the authority to notice a meeting, and members need a 20-day notice before the meeting is held.

Default rules might not be appropriate for your company, so you should not rely on them. For example, some states have a default rule that says profits should be divided equally to each member, regardless of their ownership share. It would be best to set how profits of your LLC are divided among members in your operating agreement. By drafting an operating agreement, members can be protected from liability in connection with the business the LLC conducts. Members should always try to give their LLC a separate existence. By drafting an operating agreement — together with the articles of incorporation — you are giving a life to your LLC. Without an operating agreement, an LLC may appear to be a sole proprietorship or partnership. Although you might have chosen an LLC over a corporation because there are fewer formalities, it is wise to adopt some of the same concepts.

A company's organizers must make the vital decision of how the ownership percentages of an LLC are divided. You must choose judiciously, as those with more than 50 percent of the vote can influence decisions. Often, LLC members compete for the majority vote to secure control of the company. In addition, when the LLC is sold, the more ownership percentage you have, the more assets you receive. Each owner's percentage share of the profits and losses of an LLC is known as his or her distributive share. Usually, it is equal to his or her percentage ownership share. For example, suppose Carlita is a 55 percent owner and Olive is a 45 percent owner of an LLC. At the close of the year, they earned profits of $10,000. They will divide this sum according to their respective ownership share. Carlita would get 55 percent, and her distributive share would be $5,500. Sheila would get 45 percent, and her distributive share would be $4,500.

Special allocations are defined as those that occur when profits are not divided in proportion to the percentage share, or the distributive share does not equal the percentage ownership share. Special allocations are legal, but the IRS examines them closely. They want to make sure that you are not hiding income or allocating losses to be deducted by the owner in the highest tax bracket. The rules for such special allocations are extremely complex. It is recommended that you consult an accountant or attorney to set up special allocations.

To sum up, your operating agreement should cover:

- Authority and responsibilities of members and managers
- Time and date of annual meetings of managers and members
- Routine for the election of managers
- Routine for the removal of managers for manager-managed LLCs
- Requirements for quorum for member votes
- Requirements for quorum for manager votes for manager-managed LLC
- Routine for voting by written consent when absent at a formal meeting

- Routine for giving proxies to other members

- How losses and profits will be distributed among members

- Rules for transfer of ownership when a member wants to sell ownership interest (usually called buy-sell rules)

How do you adopt your operating agreement? All members and owners of a LLC sign the agreement. Once signed, each agrees to be bound by the rules contained therein.

Step 10: Obtain an employer identification number

Because your newly created LLC is a full-fledged legal entity, you must obtain an employer identification number (EIN) as required by federal law. This number is also required to open up a bank account. Simply complete Form SS-4, Application for Employer Identification Number, or apply online. The online procedure is relatively new and can save time and energy. When you mail the form, it usually takes approximately six weeks. By faxing, it will take approximately five days. You can obtain a number immediately by calling the IRS directly, but this is only available in some states.

Tax Considerations

LLCs provide the same tax benefits to small-business owners as sole proprietorships and partnerships. Income is passed through to the owners for tax purposes. Each owner will receive the portion of income that was specified in the operating agreement. For example, if a business with two owners earned $100,000 in a tax year, and Owner 1 was to receive 60 percent, that owner would be taxed on $60,000. Owner 2 was designated to receive 40 percent and would be taxed on $40,000.

When the LLC has only one owner, taxes are handled in the same manner as with a sole proprietorship. As discussed, although sole proprietorships and partnerships offer simplicity of tax treatment, their owners are subject to personal liability for their debts. A limited partnership even must designate one member to be personally liable for its debts, though it does benefit from pass-through taxation. For these reasons, many business owners form limited liability companies that provide pass-through taxation but enjoy limited personal liability protection.

For purposes of taxation, the IRS treats a single-owner LLC like a sole proprietorship, while a multi-member LLC is treated like a partnership. No special tax forms are required for an LLC — they use the same forms as the sole proprietorship and partnership. This means that a sole proprietorship and partnership may both convert to an LLC without any change in its tax status or income-tax reporting requirements. They both would then acquire the personal limited liability protection without any problem. You may convert without owing any money to the government if you convert in this manner, unlike if you sold the assets and liabilities of a company to an existing business entity. Review this example of Billy and his bookstore:

A customer who slipped and fell on a ladder that was open in the middle of the store is suing the three partners of Billy's Used Bookstore. The owners are sure they were not negligent because they had cones surrounding the ladder, but they do not have time to fight the person in court. The trio settles the case and then decides to convert their partnership to an LLC to make sure their assets are protected from further lawsuits. They do not have to change their tax filing information, and they continue to file their Form 1065 Partnership Return.

Because LLCs are also pass-through tax entities, they must also handle the phantom income issue that affects partnerships. Like partnerships, LLCs address the issue with a distributions clause in their operating agreement that provides for an annual stipend to each owner to cover the amount he or she owes on taxes on the profits. The provision normally includes a formula permitting each owner to obtain a percentage of his or her distributed profits equal to the highest federal and state tax rates combined. To be specific, this formula is: **Member's share of allocated profits x (highest federal income tax rate + state income tax rate) = annual distribution.** Let us look at an example:

Michael is a 50 percent owner of an LLC with $100,000 net profits at the conclusion of the tax year. His share is $50,000. Let us figure that the highest individual tax rates at the federal and state level are 35 percent and 11 percent, respectively. If Michael's operating agreement has a distributions clause with the above formula, Michael will receive $23,000 ($50,000 x 46 percent). This money is allocated so that he can pay the Internal Revenue Service and state taxes on his net profits.

The formula above more than covers the end-of-the-year tax bill for several reasons:

- Most taxpayers remit an income tax rate (entitled an "effective" income tax rate) that is less than their top (marginal) maximum rate because of the way the progressive income tax brackets operate. Despite how high their total income, all taxpayers pay a lower tax rate on the initial dollars they make, up to a maximum amount. Once they earn enough to go up to the next tax bracket, they remit tax on their additional income at this level. So, despite the fact that taxpayers might pay tax at the highest rate for some of their earned money, their effective tax rate will be lower.

- Individuals can normally subtract state income taxes remitted on their federal income tax return.

- Individuals may use other deductions such as personal exemptions and credits to further decrease their tax bill.

How you report your LLC's profits or losses to the IRS depends on how many owners there are in the LLC. If you are the sole owner of the LLC, your LLC is treated as a sole proprietorship for tax purposes. You file Form 1040, Individual Tax Return, and Schedule C (Form 1040), Profit or Loss From Business. The IRS treats your LLC as a partnership if your LLC has two or more owners. You file Form 1065, Partnership Return of Income. Management must provide copies of Schedule K-1 to each owner that sets forth the LLC's distribution of income and losses to each member.

The beauty of the LLC is that both single-member and multi-member LLCs can elect to be treated as corporations for tax purposes. You simply file Form 8832, Entity Classification Election. Consult an accountant before doing this to be sure you understand all of the implications of completing this form and filing as a corporation, if you have chosen to do business as an LLC. Just as an individual must pay both state and federal taxes in most states, an LLC must report and pay taxes at the state and federal level. The forms for each state differ. Some states use the same forms for partnerships and LLCs; others do not. You must file and report taxes in your home state, the state in which you organized your LLC, and states where you have qualified to do business as a foreign business. To simplify your paperwork and your tax liabilities, you might consider organizing your LLC in your home state.

Operating an LLC

Now that you have filed your articles of organization and executed your operating agreement, your LLC is fully formed and ready for business. All of the business entities we have discussed require some degree of formality, responsibility, and administration. This chapter will discuss the day-to-day operation and management of your newly formed LLC.

Although LLCs are not as highly regulated as corporations, LLC organizers and members should not assume that there are no procedures to follow. It must follow certain formalities and keep records. LLCs normally do not demand periodic requirements, such as annual meetings. Nonetheless, they still must respect state law and their own operating agreement, in addition to maintaining records. Take a look at what LLCs do not have to do:

- Have annual meetings of members; they may elect to do so, but law does not require it.

- Select managers from time to time; managers can serve year after year until a membership vote decides to change managers.

- Have annual manager meetings; they may elect to do so, but law does not require it.

- Managers do not have to (but should) maintain a written record of all meaningful formal decisions made during the course of doing business.

On the other hand, LLCs should observe the following formalities:

- They should have an updated operating agreement that lists the capital contributions and percentage ownership shares of each member.

- They should give proper notice of a meeting to all members of an LLC.

- They should record all votes of LLC members in written minutes, whether these votes have been cast by written consent or at a formal meeting, and maintain such minutes with the LLC's records.

- They must file periodic information reports with the secretary of state in the state where they have organized, in addition to any state where they are registered to do business.

- They must pay all annual state franchise taxes, if necessary.

- They must file annual tax reports with the IRS and in each state they conduct business.

- Their members must not engage in any activities that represent a conflict of interest when conducting business.

Meetings

Because LLCs do not have to legally hold annual meetings, they generally do not do so unless the operating agreement stipulates that they should hold them. If they do want to hold them, members must call for one. This call to a meeting is analogous to a corporation's special meeting. One purpose of such a meeting may be to remove or add managers. In any case, a call to meeting requires certain formalities.

The member (or members) calling the meeting must possess a minimum percentage of an LLC's outstanding shares; this amount differs from state to state and operating agreement to operating agreement, but it is normally 5 to 10 percent. Therefore, if a member owns less than 10 percent and wants to call a meeting, he or she must join with other owners until their collective shares total the minimum percentage.

If the LLC is a manager-managed LLC, the owner underwrites a written order to the other managers, entitled to a call for a meeting. After that, the manager(s) are responsible for sending notice of the meeting to all LLC members. If the LLC is member-managed, it does not need to issue a call to the managers, but instead just notices the members themselves. Thus, either the manager or the owner prepares notice of the meeting. Notice of the meeting must be delivered to all members advising them what proposals are to be discussed.

Appointed-manager meetings are held more informally. They conduct meetings among themselves; they do not have to adopt resolutions or document every detail that arises during the day-to-day operations of the LLC. On the other hand, significant transactions — like the purchase of real estate or closing down a division — will necessitate a meeting of the managers. The procedures for calling a meeting and noticing a meeting replicate the procedures described above for member meetings.

A written authorization by one member giving another member the right to vote for his or her shares is known as a proxy. Rules for proxies are normally described in state law and in the operating agreement. Often proxies are used when a member cannot attend a meeting but wants his or her votes to be counted. He or she then grants his or her votes to a person who attends the meeting and votes those shares on his or her behalf. Managers should not vote by proxy at manager meetings. Doing so is in violation of his or her responsibility to govern properly and to make objective decisions based on sufficient information. Proxies can last an extended period of time and so state that time in writing. If no duration is declared, the proxy lapses automatically by state law.

Member and manager meetings must be recorded. These written recordings of the events taken at meetings are called minutes. Minutes are extremely simple and concise;

they should be written in reader-friendly language with a conversational tone. Minutes of meetings normally contain the following:

- Type of meeting — Whether is it a managers' meeting or members' meeting
- Whether the meeting was called by notice or such a notice was waived
- Those in attendance
- Time, date, and location of the meeting
- Chairperson's name
- Actions taken — For example: election of directors, purchase of real estate
- Signature by person recording meeting witnessing to their accuracy

Written consents preclude the necessity of meetings and are used when members and managers take an action without a meeting. It is a formal written document that establishes a resolution or action to be instituted and is executed by the members or managers agreeing to the action. It should be written in a reader-friendly and conversational tone. Some members prefer written consent because they are faster, easier, less expensive, and more convenient. Actions taken by written consent do not have to be recorded as minutes because the written consent memorializes the action in writing. In some states, written consents must be unilateral for some LLC actions, such as the election of managers or the amendment of the articles of organization. A written consent should include the following:

- Type of action

- Declaration that the members or managers waived notice of the meeting

- Actions taken — For example, purchase of real estate, election of managers, or revision of operating agreement

- Signature line for each voting member or manager of the action's vote

The membership ledger and transfer of shares

The membership ledger is the vital record that you will keep for your LLC. It is simply a registry listing the members who own the LLC, the percentage interest each possesses, and the transfers or other management changes of such ownership. Upon formation of the LLC, all LLCs should institute the ledger and should conscientiously update the ledger when ownership is transferred, gifted, sold, repurchased by the members, or new units are issued.

Remember, the Securities and Exchange Commission (SEC) and other state and federal authorities regulate company shares. Some shares, called registered shares, are publicly traded shares sold in the public market like the stock exchange. Therefore, if you dispose of shares in a nonpublic company, follow the exemptions allowed by state and federal law. Contact the state securities department in your state to determine the appropriate regulations and exemptions.

Requirements for annual reporting

Most states demand LLCs to submit periodic reports to the secretary of state's office. Some states, such as California and Alaska, only require LLCs to be filed every two years. Check with your secretary of state. Some states like Georgia, California, and Arkansas offer online filing of periodic reports. It can be expected that more states will join the group soon. States differ regarding their filing requirements, filing fees, due dates, and late penalties.

Amending articles of organization and operating agreement

Members are allowed to amend the LLC's articles of organization and operating agreement. They have the right and power to vote on proposed amendments at a called meeting. Conversely, the members may approve an amendment by written consent. Nevertheless, all amendments to the articles of organization must be filed with the secretary of state. Most states even provide a form exclusively for that purpose. Nonetheless, the amendment to the articles of organization will not be effective until the secretary of state approves it. Some states require a supermajority or unanimous vote before they will approve it.

Common amendments are as follows:

- Changing the name of the LLC
- Changing the LLC's business purpose
- Adopting an additional class of units

If any of these amendments are approved, the appropriate paperwork will then have to be filed with the state to notify it of the legal changes. Similarly, members also have the right to amend an LLC's operating agreement. The procedure for doing so is described in your operating agreement. Because operating agreements are not legal documents, the amendments to the operating agreement do not have to be filed with the secretary of state. They are effective immediately upon the completion of the members or managers.

Advantages and disadvantages

The advantages of an LLC are similar to those of a corporation. The members of an LLC incur financial risk only in the amount of the investment in the LLC. Because of this, it is easier to obtain investors to this form of business entity than to a partnership. Members can enjoy the profits of the company and tax deductions of the LLC but will divide fewer of the financial risks. Another one of its advantages is similar to partnerships — pass-through tax status. Members' profits and deductions will pass through to his or her individual tax return, as the LLC is not taxed in and of itself.

LLCs also offer flexibility in management. It can be run by members/owners or by managers who are not members or owners. Thus, hands-on owners or members or hired non-member managers can manage it. This affords owners the choice of who should run the company if they feel someone outside of the ownership has expertise in his or her field. The LLC also offers flexibility in how profits and losses are distributed to members. Unlike corporations, an

LLC member may be allocated 50 percent of the profits, even if he or she only contributed 20 percent of the start-up capital.

One of the LLC's disadvantages is similar to that of a partnership. Because it is managed like a partnership, the possibility of internal conflict among members exists. Another disadvantage of an LLC is that state law regulates it — they do not have the ease of formation of sole proprietorships or partnerships. LLCs are more complex than sole proprietorships or partnerships, even though they share some similarities, especially in their form of taxation. The paperwork required for an LLC is more than for a general partnership but still less than for a corporation. As a result, LLC owners are subject to more regulation from the state than a sole proprietorship or partnership would be. All states require a fee for establishing the company; some states also require annual fees, which can run into several hundred dollars, for the ongoing existence of an LLC.

Similar to partnerships and sole proprietorships, LLCs do not have the quality of continuity. They do not exist outside of the owners and, therefore, if the owners die, the LLC ceases to exist. But this is changing. Recently, states have permitted LLCs to exist in perpetuity, though the lines are blurry. There still may be problems if the sole member of the LLC becomes disabled or perishes. These problems can be ameliorated by stipulating in the articles of organization of the limited liability company that upon the death or disability of the owner of the LLC, the heirs or estate of the member automatically become members of the company. Finally, like partnerships, it may be hard to transfer ownership or sell interest in an LLC to another entity should you want out of the company.

Foreign LLCs

LLC businesses that transact business in a state other than the state where they are organized are considered a foreign business in that state and operate as a guest. Transacting business as a foreign business in that state may require you to register your business in that state. For example, a Florida business that sells products in California must register as a foreign business with the secretary of state in California and register with Florida's secretary of state. After that, the Florida LLC must file periodic reports with the secretary of state in California for as long as it transacts business in California. *More details about doing business in other states will be discussed in Chapter 8.*

This process of registering as a foreign LLC is known as qualification. Remember, the criteria for what constitutes doing business in a state varies from state to state. In California, a single transaction constitutes doing business there. Check the state's LLC statutes for more specific information. *A list of state Web sites is provided in the Appendix.*

Businesses That Can Take Advantage of LLCs

In previous chapters, we have discussed each business structure with its features, advantages, and disadvantages. Now, let us discuss your decision to choose an LLC by looking closely at which businesses may benefit from this popular business entity.

Companies with few active members: An LLC provides all owners with limited liability protection and full executive power in management decisions, so member-managed LLCs work best with businesses with a small number of members. It is possible, though, to have a larger LLC with a select few being active in management, depending upon its structure. In this case, the larger LLC would require more paperwork, which defeats the purpose of the ease of management. As a rule of thumb, companies with more than 15 or 20 owners should form a corporation instead of an LLC.

Businesses that want to divide profits and losses in a flexible manner without the extra level of corporate income tax: LLC owners can divide profits and losses the way they want to — regardless of their capital interest and subject to special IRS specifications — without having to deal with the corporate income tax. If they do earn more money and want to shield it from higher income taxes, they can choose the corporate income tax treatment for the LLC. In addition, if they want to shelter the money or keep it in the company, they can select this same corporate income tax option.

Start-up businesses: New businesses first starting out often lose money the first couple of years. To protect themselves, new businesses often form LLCs because the income lost can be deducted from the earnings made from a second job or money earned from investments. LLCs enable owners to deduct losses from the business from their total earned income on their individual tax return.

Uninsured businesses: If you do not carry insurance against liability resulting from such occurrences as slip-fall, defective merchandise, bad debt, and any other matter that can arise in the course of doing business, LLCs provide limited liability protection to your personal assets. The best way to do this is to form an LLC; if you want to raise money or go public, a corporation is the best choice.

General partnerships or sole proprietorships: If you are a sole proprietor or a member in a general partnership and someone sues you, your personal assets can be seized. Sole proprietorships, as previously discussed, are the easiest and most convenient way to start up a business. There is no paperwork involved, and your income is reported on your individual tax return. Nevertheless, one lawsuit can not only put you out of business, but also cause you to lose your personal assets and go bankrupt. Your business may be booming now, but you should protect yourself in case a lawsuit wipes you out. To change to an LLC, you do not even have to change your tax status; you continue to report on 1040 Schedule C. The same thing goes for general partnerships. It may be an easy and convenient way to start a business, but you never know when you will be liable for a judgment or bad debt. If you are a general partnership and decided to change to an LLC, you continue to file your 1065 partnership return. All you have to do to convert to an LLC is fill out the LLC articles, pay a fee, and file them with the state.

Businesses considering forming an S corporation: The LLC was designed to replace the S corporation, even though a business can still opt to become an S corporation. Members get the same limited liability protection and a more beneficial form of pass-through tax treatment.

Businesses That May Not Take Advantage of an LLC Entity

Companies with no risk of liability or business debt: If you are starting a business alone where you do not anticipate incurring any high debt or liability, then it is best to remain a sole proprietorship. For example, if you are a freelance editor, you do not have any vendors or suppliers to pay, nor do you have a high risk of being sued. For this reason, it does not make sense to form an LLC and complicate matters further. In addition, if you do not have to raise capital for your business in the form of a loan, you should not form an LLC. For example, if you are a freelance creative consultant, you normally work for yourself, where you do not incur much debt — nor do you need to raise significant amounts of capital because you have limited overhead expenses. It is unlikely that you will be sued, so you do not need the limited liability protection that the LLC affords. In summary, if you are self-employed in a business that has little or no risk of taking on liability or building debt, you should keep your life as simple as possible and remain a sole proprietor.

Professional companies: As we discussed previously, in some states — such as California — professionals are prohibited from forming LLCs. In these cases, an RLLP may better shield you from personal liability in the case of malpractice suits against other members of your firm.

Businesses seeking capital and IPOs to go public: If your firm intends to obtain large-scale capital from investors or wants to go public on the stock exchange via initial public offerings (IPOs), the corporation is your best option. This also holds true for companies wishing to offer employees stock option plans.

CASE STUDY: FORMING AN LLC

David Cheatham
Transform Communications LLC
Web site: www.transform-
communications.com

My business focuses on strategic communications consultancy. I launched the business to build on many years of corporate experience in the communications field. I started Transform Communications LLC to provide a special service to organizations across the supply chain, namely to help them navigate change.

When forming my new business, I considered which business entity would work best for my type of business. I chose the LLC because of the ease, speed, and flexibility in setting it up and operating it. The LLC is a straightforward business structure and is the form used by most of my consulting colleagues.

Although I did face some challenges when planning and launching my business, namely proving the business case, niche, and differentiators, I have had no issues in regard to my choice of the LLC as a business structure.

I would recommend that an aspiring new business owner consult with a small business attorney when researching the legal entity options available.

Chapter 6
Corporations

P erhaps you have an LLC, partnership, or sole proprietorship that is doing well, and you want to grow your
business. Or maybe you want to raise capital with an eye
to the future. For these reasons, a corporation may be the
right structure to consider. The corporation has its advantages and disadvantages, including a built-in liability
shield and some tax advantages. Once you have decided
to form a corporation, you will go through the steps listed
below. First, take a look at an overview of what to expect.

General Overview

Paperwork is one of the operative terms to forming a corporation, which begins with the articles of incorporation.
You will also have to pay a filing fee for filing the articles of
incorporation. Corporate liability protection and tax benefits begin upon completion and submission of your articles of incorporation and fees. The articles of incorporation
include standard information like the name and address
of the corporate entity, who will be its manager, and the
amount and type of stock it will issue. Small corporations
begin with common stock where each share of stock equals

one vote. The fee for filing articles of incorporation is approximately $100 or less.

Next, owners should complete the bylaws of the corporation. The bylaws describe the duties and rights of the directors or managers, the owners or shareholders, and the officers of the corporation. Bylaws also describe when annual meetings between shareholders or owners and directors or managers will take place.

A corporation may have only one owner or shareholder, according to states' laws. He or she can be both the sole shareholder and the sole director. In several states, that person may also fill the officer positions, such as president, treasurer, and secretary, as required. A few states require you to establish two different people to fill the officer positions. Some states expect a minimum number of directors based on the number of shareholders. For example, if you have two shareholders, you must have two directors, and so on. Unlike an LLC, a corporation cannot have a business as its corporate director — it must be an individual.

Corporations and LLCs are considered chartered entities. Unlike sole proprietorships and partnerships, submitting a charter document in the state where it is formed creates the corporation. In this case, its charter document is the articles of incorporation. Corporations are regulated by the state and have a definite structure. These two features are often turn-offs to the budding entrepreneur. Remember, though, that corporations in the United States and abroad own and control a great part of the world's resources.

Corporation management

One does not have to be a shareholder of a corporation to be its manager. Managers are often appointed; this is called representative management. The managers are elected by shareholders who vote for the board of directors at the annual meeting. The board of directors is the ruling body of a corporation. The board of directors also elects officers such as a president, chief executive officer (CEO), secretary, chief financial officer (CFO), treasurer, and vice president. These officers run the corporation. Sometimes members of the board of directors wear two hats, serving as officers of the corporation as well.

The board of directors takes action in a formal manner; their actions are officially documented by minutes and take place at meetings where notices are posted for all to review. On the contrary, officers operate the corporation on a less formal basis and are responsible for its day-to-day functions. Officers do not require a vote to take action.

The board of directors of a corporation has the power and responsibility to:

- Issue new shares of stock
- Finalize long-term planning
- Finalize the distribution of real estate or other titled property
- Finalize the buying of other businesses
- Finalize any mergers or consolidations with other businesses

The officers of a corporation have the power and responsibility to:

- Manage the company on a day-to-day basis
- Hire and terminate employees
- Requisition office supplies and finalize purchases
- Pay bills
- Perform sales and collect account receivables

Because corporations have representative management like the U.S. government, they must have rules by which to govern. The bylaws are those rules governing the internal operation of the corporation.

A C corporation is simply a for-profit corporation, which is the umbrella form of all corporations; the "C" is derived from the chapter of the IRS regulations that determine the tax regulations involved with the corporation. A C corporation is a separate entity, according to the legal and tax definition, and is treated as a separate entity, particularly in regard to determining taxes.

S Corporation

S corporations are taxed on a pass-through basis, just like partnerships. An S corporation also qualifies for the limited liability protection of the corporation. The S corporation is similar to an LLC.

The S corporation is formed in the same manner as a C corporation — it files articles of incorporation and pays state filing fees. Though, to become an S corporation, shareholders have to sign and file an S corporation tax election, Form 2253, Election by a Small Business Corporation; this is a tax, not a legal issue. The S corporation is bound by the same legal rules as a C corporation.

LLCs have mostly replaced S corporations. Before LLCs, S corporations were the only business entity that afforded liability protection and also pass-through taxation that would avoid the double taxation of regular or C corporations). Whereas LLCs offer the same benefits as S corporations, S corporations have some restrictions. No more than 100 shareholders are permitted in an S corporation. These shareholders must be U.S. citizens or residents or have specific trusts or estates. Although the 100-member restriction does not affect many companies — most small businesses have three to five owners — the citizen/resident restriction might be a problem.

Under the Internal Revenue Code and state corporate tax statutes, an S corporation is taxed on a pass-through basis. The pass-through status of the S corporation means that the profits, losses, and deductions of the business pass through to the corporation's shareholders, proportional to their ownership shares in the business. For example, a 20 percent shareholder reports 20 percent of the net earnings or debits on his or her individual tax return. The corporation as an entity does not pay income taxes on its earnings. An S corporation must meet certain tax requirements. Two of the most important tax requirements are:

- **S corporations have one class of stock only.** An S corporation cannot underwrite preferred classes of stocks to investors. They also cannot set up profit-

and-loss sharing ratios among the owners who are not in direct proportion to their percentage of stock ownership. In an S corporation, earnings and proceeds from liquidation must be distributed in proportion to each owner relative to his or her ownership interest in the corporation.

- **S corporations have limitations on ownership.** Besides spouses and other family members who count as one shareholder, S corporations may have only up to 100 shareholders, and they all must be U.S. citizens or permanent residents. This limitation is fine for a privately held corporation, but it is limiting for a publicly held corporation, where shareholders normally exceed 100. Moreover, nonresident aliens, and other business entities, may not be S corporation shareholders. These restrictions should be taken into account if you want to do international. Also, the fact that other businesses may not own stock in your business also limits your sources of capital.

You do not have to be incorporated to make an S corporation tax election. Partnerships and LLCs can elect to be considered a C corporation, without converting your business. Simply file Form 8832, Entity Classification Election. After an unincorporated business selects corporate tax status, it can then select S corporation tax treatment if it adheres to the regulations. Obviously, it is not really sensible to perform this two-step process to achieve the pass-through tax status you have in the first place, unless you seek to lower your self-employment taxes, which are owed each year on profits allocated to business owners. Consult your tax adviser for more details on this procedure.

Effects on finances and taxes of an S corporation tax election

Let us examine the effects on finances and taxes of converting from a C corporation to an S corporation. First, consider the advantages:

Advantage: Profits pass through the business to owners. Converting a C corporation to an S corporation can be a convenient way to pass earnings and losses through to owners over several years. If the corporation changes to an LLC to obtain the same result, both the corporation and the individual owners may have to remit taxes.

For example: Shane and Mark, owners of Spiral Software, a start-up software business, form a corporation to acquire financing. They acquire money from Shane in exchange for a sizable amount of common stock and a seat on the board. Shane demands the company elect an S corporation during the business's early tax years. He wants to deduct the losses from the business to offset gains from other investments on his tax return. Then, when the corporation starts making money, he wants the profits distributed to him and others instead of being locked in the corporation and taxed at corporate rates. Mark hopes to end the S corporation tax election once the business starts making more money, or if the corporation issues a second class of preferred stock to a capital venture fund, which is not allowed for an S corporation.

Note: Switching back and forth between a C corporation and an S corporation status can create tax complications, as it might raise suspicions as to your motives for doing so. There are rules governing the amount of income earned and passed through to S corporation shareholders after the conversion to S corporation status. Ask your tax advisor about accumulated adjustments accounts.

Advantage: Just one level of tax must be paid when the S corporation is sold or dissolved. After an S corporation is sold or liquidated, just the shareholders remit tax — not the corporation itself. On the other hand, when a C corporation is sold, both the shareholders and the corporation pay taxes. Shareholders only pay taxes in excess of the value of their basis in corporate stock — the price they paid for the stock. This tax break is good only if the S corporation did not operate as a C corporation within 10 years of the date of liquidation when its assets appreciated. This situation should encourage you to convert a C corporation to an S corporation before corporate assets grow.

For example: Time Realty Inc., owned by Robin and Linda, selected the S corporation option soon after it was incorporated. Upon dissolution, the corporation sells its tangible property for $150,000. The corporation's basis in this real estate values at $70,000, so it has a net gain of $80,000 on the purchase. Half of this increase ($40,000) is distributed to each of the shareholders and taxed on their respective individual income tax returns at long-term capital gain rates. Assume that each owner has a basis of $35,000. The passed-through $40,000 of S corporation gain raises the basis each shareholder has to $75,000 ($40,000 + $35,000). Each shareholder received $75,000 for the liquidation of the corporation — half of the $150,000 proceeds from the sale. Robin and Linda do not owe any more tax when they obtain the proceeds. They would owe only when the proceeds are more than their income tax basis in the shares. In this case, their basis is identical to the total sum, so this is a tax-free transaction.

Advantage: S corporations result in lower self-employment taxes. Profits paid out to shareholders in an S corporation are not subject to self-employment taxes. Profits paid out as salaries to the owners are subject to self-employment taxes. This can be a benefit to the S corporation owner who, unlike his or her active LLC owners, must pay self-employment tax on all profits of the business.

For example: Ron owns Unique Screw Corp., a company that manufactures see-through plastic screws for electronic components. Because federal individual income tax rates are lower and self-employment tax rates are higher than when he began, Ron seeks all corporate profits to pass through his company to him. Ron receives a $100,000 salary, and any remaining profits he puts back into the corporation. Ron's tax adviser, Gail, tells him to make an S corporation tax election and decrease his corporate salary to $60,000. The remaining profits that normally go to Ron will not be subject to self-employment tax, although his $60,000 will. Gail tells Ron that if he decreases his salary more, he may raise a red flag with the IRS as a social security tax evasion case. If the IRS can prove that Ron's salary is lower than average, the IRS can make Ron remit self-employment tax on the amount of salary it thinks he should earn, with additional penalties and interest. Gail also suggests amending the corporation's bylaws to necessitate the distribution of all net profits to the corporation's shareholders at the end of each fiscal tax year. By doing this, Ron receives all remaining profits (after remittance of his salary and other expenses) free and clear of self-employment tax.

Note: Most business owners do not choose an S corporation to lower their self-employment taxes. They feel it is not worth incurring the suspicion of the IRS and consider paying social security as one of the day-to-day expenses of owning and operating a business.

Disadvantage: S corporations that were previously C corporations may lose their status as S corporations if they make surplus passive income, which is rents, royalties, dividends, interest, and similar sources. Under some technicalities, a business can lose its status as an S corporation if it operated as a C corporation and made earnings and profits that were inherited by the S corporation. In addition, if the S corporation earns 25 percent more of its income from passive income sources for three straight years, the S corporation may lose its status as an S corporation.

Disadvantage: S corporations are allowed to deduct fewer losses than other business entities with pass-through tax treatment. However, S corporate shareholders are more limited insofar as deducting debt to reduce tax bills. Debt includes money borrowed by the business or debts suffered by the corporation in connection with the buying of property, such as a mortgage on real estate owned by the corporation. The tax rules regarding the above are extremely technical, but rest assured that you would be more limited in your right to deduct such corporate debt from your tax basis than a sole proprietor, partnership, or LLC.

Be advised that for newly created companies, an LLC is a more preferable option than an S corporation. If you wish to form a small, privately held business with limited liability protection and pass-through tax treatment, an LLC is a better choice than forming a corporation and electing an S corporation option. In addition to being simpler to form and keep, an LLC can be owned by individuals and entities and has few ownership limitations. It also affords better chances for its owners to increase their tax basis by using debt as deductions.

S corporation election

File IRS Form 2553, Election by a Small Business Corporation, to make an S corporation tax election. After you select S corporation tax status, the corporation must submit an S corporation information tax form, IRS Form 1120S, U.S. Income Tax Return for an S Corporation. The corporation must also complete a Schedule K-1 (Form 1120S), Shareholder's Share of Income, Credits, Deductions, for each shareholder that reveals the distributed profits, losses, and other deductions and credits that get passed through to each shareholder at the conclusion of the fiscal year.

The S corporation status ends when the corporation stops meeting the S corporation eligibility requirements, such as bringing on shareholders that are not U.S. citizens or are other business entities. S corporations will also end when a majority of shareholders consent to revoking it. When an S corporation is selected and then terminated or revoked, it cannot re-elect S corporation status for five years.

Capital for a Corporation

A corporation is normally chosen as the best entity for which to raise initial capital. Institutional investors and lenders and venture capitalists prefer to fund corporations because they know their investment is protected legally. Sole proprietorships, for example, are required to file very little paperwork, and that is mostly to be registered to do business in their local city or county. On the other hand, a corporation has organized directors, created and filed articles of incorporation, and worked through the necessary steps to generate the legal protection that allows investors recourse to recoup their investments. Investors and financial institutions are simply more comfortable knowing that extensive paperwork has been generated and filed, particularly if it is paperwork that will help protect them.

Stock options and warrants — stock options underwritten to an investor or lender to buy stock at a fixed price — are additional corporate vehicles that interest private capital sources seeking to invest in a business with good potential. Corporate stock options and warrants guarantee the sale of additional shares at a fixed price to lenders and investors. In a type of domino effect, if the corporation uses the initial funds paid or loaned by the firm wisely and the worth of the corporation's shares increase, the investor can then take advantage of this success by buying more shares at the negotiated option or warrant price (which will usually be less than the market price of the appreciated shares).

It is possible to tailor an LLC operating agreement to contain such investment strategies, but it would be costly in terms of legal fees. Besides, most investors feel more comfortable with the tax strategies provided to corporations under the Internal Revenue Code, rather than the more lenient tax structure of the LLC.

Public offerings

As we have said, corporations have the advantage over all other business entities because they can sell ownership interests to the public. Moreover, the securities industry and its laws specifically regulate the public acquisition of shares. For example, standard commercial and securities laws regulate the offering, sale, and transfer of stock shares. And most shareholders are aware that they will divide in proportion the dividends and worth of the corporation they buy into. This comprises the essence of a stockholder's interest in the corporation.

This does not hold true for an LLC investment or unincorporated business entity because the marketability and nature of such business entities are not as certain. LLCs' and partnerships' procedures for splitting profits, losses, voting power, and liquidation of assets are done in disproportionate ways, and investors would have to carefully examine the rights and restrictions of the company.

Unlike pass-through business entities, the fact that corporations do not automatically distribute earnings and profits to investors is another reason why corporations are effective vehicles for public offerings. Corporate profits are only distributed and taxed to investors when the board of directors declares a dividend, and dividends, unlike the earnings of unincorporated businesses, must be allocated once the board directs it to do so. In other words, a corporate shareholder who receives dividends pays taxes on only that dividend — not on phantom income that may be kept in the business's bank account.

13 Steps to Incorporation

You have decided you want to incorporate your business. Let us look at the players directly involved in the process. The incorporator is the individual or business structure that organizes the corporation, edits and files the articles of incorporation, finalizes bylaws, and selects the directors. They normally are able to initiate action before the board of directors is elected.

His or her powers are extensive at the outset of incorporating the business. Once the incorporator's initial tasks are completed, the corporation is organized and directors are selected; the directors then undertake the supervision of the corporation, and the function of incorporator ceases. When you choose a lawyer to form your corporation, he or she becomes the incorporator on your behalf. If you form the corporation yourself, you become the incorporator.

The other key player in the creation of your corporation is the secretary of state. The secretary of state is the state authority responsible for receiving and archiving all legal documents, inclusive of your corporation papers. The name of the department may vary. For example, Hawaii has a Department of Commerce and Consumer Affairs and Arizona has a Corporation Commission. Yet, each deals in corporate filings and falls under the auspices of the secretary of state.

Initially, one of the first steps in the formation of the corporation is to file your articles of incorporation with the secretary of the state. The articles of incorporation will officially launch your business. You will then be dealing with the secretary of state quite often as your corporation's business operations progress. On an ongoing basis, you must then submit annual reports and records to the secretary of state's office. You will not be required to submit your bylaws or meeting minutes. If you do not pay taxes or do not submit your corporation's required periodic reports, the secretary of state may withdraw your corporation's good standing status. If this happens, your corporation will be issued an administrative dissolution, essentially ending the life of the corporation. Each state's laws regarding this delinquency vary. Nonetheless, if this happens, your personal liability protection may be rescinded. *A listing of the secretary of state's offices for all states is provided in the Appendix.*

Once you have decided to form a business corporation, you will need to follow these 13 steps to ensure that the processes and the paperwork are all in good order, and that your new business is a solid legal entity.

Step 1: Decide where to incorporate

Before filing the articles of incorporation, you must decide where you want to incorporate — which state is the best for you to incorporate in. Take into account the following factors:

- State or states where you do business
- State taxation
- Amount of corporate filing fees
- Fees for annual filings and requirements for annual reporting
- Advantages intrinsic to certain states, such as privacy rights and directors' rights

If you have a small business and you do business in only one state, you should incorporate in that state. States normally demand foreign corporations to pay fees and register in the state in which they do business. As we discussed earlier in the book, registration in a foreign state is often known as qualification. If you plan to do business in other states, you will need to be sure that all of the appropriate paperwork, with the required fees, has been filed in those states.

Yet, if you conduct business in many states or expect to expand as your business grows, then you should be selective and choose the state that is most beneficial to you. The most popular state for incorporation has traditionally been Delaware, mainly because it offers lower corporate taxation than the other states. Delaware has a large industry that serves corporations that have filed there.

The benefits of incorporating in Delaware are:

- Inexpensive franchise tax — $35 for most businesses

- Liberal laws to shield directors from personal liability resulting from their actions

- A separate court system — the Court of Chancery — that deals in corporate issues

- Corporations are allowed to conduct business with a great deal of anonymity

- No minimum capital investment needed to form a corporation

- Its Division of Corporations is accessible by telephone

- Incorporation can be offered within a few hours for a special fee

The disadvantages of a Delaware corporation are:

- Low franchise tax, but the form you need to complete is extremely complicated and confusing

- Poor Web site support (For example, you cannot do a search for existing corporations on their Web site because they do not have a database. This would be problematic when trying to name your corporation)

Nevada is also a favorable state in which to incorporate. The advantages of a Nevada corporation are:

- Low corporate taxes (even lower than Delaware's), no corporate income tax, no tax on shares, and no franchise tax

- Liberal laws to protect directors from personal liability resulting from their actions

- Corporations can act with a great deal of privacy and anonymity

- No information-sharing agreement with the IRS

- Excellent customer service and Web support

The disadvantages of Nevada corporations are:

- Must name your directors when articles of incorporation are submitted

- Expensive incorporation fees — Among the highest in the nation

- Must remit an annual $85 fee along with the annual report of officers

- Bad reputation of companies incorporating doing illicit actives, such as laundering money

Step 2: Select your corporate name

After deciding on where you wish to incorporate, the next step is selecting your corporate name. Remember, you may use a trade, but you must file a DBA (doing business as) form with your county clerk for using a fictitious name.

As discussed at the beginning of the book, the most important detail to know when selecting a corporate name is to make sure that no other person or business entity currently has the same name. There are two operative factors going on here. First, your use of their name may impose on their trademark or service mark rights. This could result in legal problems. Second, the secretary of state's office will not register your corporation if its name is already being utilized. You may ask the difference between a trademark and a service mark is. They are really basically one and the same thing, except service marks refer to a service and trademarks refer to a product. In either case, it is advisable to search for existing trademarks and corporate names to determine whether your selected name is in use.

To search for registered and pending trademarks at the U.S. Patent and Trademark Office Web, go to **www.uspto.com. gov/web/menu/tm.html**; there, you can use the Trademark Electronic Search System (TESS). Go to the New User Form Search and type in the name you want to use. Then click "Search Term." Be certain that the "Field" term is on "Combined Word Mark." You will want to conduct a comprehensive search, as there may be names that are similar to yours that you will also want to be able to find. To ensure you are covering all of the bases, you should:

- Enter all phonetically similar names of your company because names that are phonetically similar can cause conflicts in trademark use.

- Enter the singular and the plural of your company's proposed name.

- If your proposed name has more than one word, enter each word separately.

- Read and adhere to the instructions for the usage of "wild-card" search terms. This generally means adding an asterisk (*) after the first few letters of a word.

Again, just because nothing appears in the USPTO database does not mean you are free and clear for using that name. You will find only registered names, and there may be unregistered business names that are in use as well. These unregistered names would be considered valid trademarks, even though they may not show up in the United States Patent and Trademark office database. So, you should also do a broader Internet search for your proposed name to find additional companies that may be using your proposed name. If, through these searches, you have not discovered any conflicting trademarks or service marks, you should then search the secretary of state's records for existing corporate names. Most states offer free searches of existing corporate names; contact the secretary of state in the state in which you plan on incorporating online or by phone to begin your search.

When you are certain that your proposed name is available for use, you may want to reserve it. This step is not absolutely necessary. Most states offer a reservation service where you file a short name reservation form with the secretary of state. However, you should also be aware that there is usually a fee for this service. When you have finalized your name, make sure that you have an appropriate corporate suffix:

- Corporation or Corp.
- Incorporated or Inc.

Step 3: Choose the type of corporation

You will need to determine whether your business will be formed as a C corporation or an S corporation. As discussed before, the main differences involve tax liabilities. The process of incorporation is the same for both types. You will need to file your articles of incorporation and pay the appropriate fee. However, at this point in your business startup, you will need to choose between a C and an S corporation.

Step 4: Select the registered agent

What is a registered agent for a corporation? Similar to the registered agent used to form an LLC, a corporation's registered agent is an individual who has the authority and is empowered and responsible for receiving legal documentation on behalf of the company. The articles of incorporation identify the registered agent, but filing a notice with the secretary of state's office can change this. Although the corporation exists in perpetuity and has a life of its own, it is not a physical person and needs to designate an individual or entity to receive business and legal documentation on its behalf. Fees for such agents — known also as the agent for service of process, local agent, and resident agent — are modest. You should not pay more than $75 annually, although prices generally range from $50 to $350. They usually work closely with the secretary of state's office in the state where you plan to incorporate so they can answer questions about fees, procedures, and the forms or applications.

The registered agent need not be an outsider. It can be you, a relative, or your attorney. It can also be a company that specializes in corporation services. Remember, the registered agent is a matter of public record. Therefore, if you wish to remain anonymous, then hire a professional. The agent must have an address in the state of incorporation. Therefore, if you live in New York and incorporated as a Delaware corporation, you must find an agent in the state of Delaware.

Hiring an attorney or professional company to serve as your agent has its benefits. They are stable and have long-term addresses. Not only that, but they are also likely to understand the nature of the papers served upon you. They will also receive other government mailings like tax forms, annual corporate report forms, legal notices and other documentation related to your business. Also, do not use a post office box number as an address for your agent. First, some states prohibit it, and second, you may never receive the legal papers.

Step 5: Decide to do it yourself or hire an attorney

Now that you have decided on where to incorporate and successfully chosen a name, you should think about whether you want to incorporate yourself, use a discount incorporation service, or hire an attorney. There are advantages and disadvantages to each.

The benefit of incorporating yourself is that you will save money. However, unless you are comfortable with the process and truly understand the legal ramifications involved in preparing and filing the paperwork required to form your corporation — paperwork that can become extremely detailed and complicated — you may find that spending the money for qualified legal assistance would be a wise investment.

A discount incorporation service is another alternative. They cost between $200 and $300 per incorporation and cover the following:

- Submitting of articles of incorporation
- Selecting the type of corporation
- Drafting of bylaws
- Drafting of minutes of organizational meetings of directors

You must perform the following functions if you choose a discount incorporation service:

- Writing and revising bylaws
- Looking at and revising minutes for organizational meeting of directors
- Holding the organizational meeting of directors
- Issuing stock
- Complying with state securities laws
- Submitting initial corporate reports and periodic reports

You do, nonetheless, receive value for your dollar. They cut through red tape and are efficient with their filings. Still, there are some blanks in the boilerplate bylaws and minutes that they prepare, and they may make mistakes.

If your new corporation has one or two owners, self-incorporation is recommended. Yet, if you have several owners, you may want to hire a business attorney. When the number of owners is large, incorporation becomes more complex, and the legal and financial consequences can have significantly more impact on your business operations. A qualified business attorney does the following:

- Foresees problems as well as viable solutions

- Helps with complex aspects of business organizations, such as shareholder agreements

- Prepares bylaws and minutes of directors' meetings tailored to your specifications

- Ensures the corporation is in compliance with securities laws (both state and federal) when interests in the business are sold to raise capital

Networking is often the best option for finding a qualified lawyer to help with incorporating your business. You can also check with your local bar association for a list of qualified lawyers who specialize in business incorporations. When deciding on a lawyer, do not base your decision on cost alone. Incorporating your business can become quite challenging. Avoiding legal and financial problems can be well worth the money spent on a qualified, experienced attorney who can help you manage the paperwork involved.

Step 6: Select the stock structure

As a part of creating a corporation, owners are issued shares of stock, which designate the corporation ownership. This is known as equity. You must select stock structure in the planning stages of your corporation because you must include it in your articles of incorporation.

Each shareholder who has entered into the corporation should sign an investment representation letter. The letter protects the corporation, as it spells out and verifies that the shareholder agrees to the risk he or she will assume and his or her qualifications to serve as a shareholder of the corporation by taking on a percentage of the ownership. He or she also includes in the letter his or her investment objectives, which are essential to comply with state and federal securities laws. Similar to an LLC, corporations may also have additional stock classes. There are three additional classes of stock: common, preferred, and hybrid.

Common stock is simply referred to as plain voting stock. All corporations are required to have at least one class of voting stock. The most common class is the voting common stock. A class of voting stock is essential because if the shareholders cannot vote for a board of directors to govern the corporation, the corporation cannot take any legal action and thus ceases to exist.

Preferred stock refers to stock that gives stockholders monetary entitlement over another class of shares. Normally, this means that preferred stockholders receive priority in getting their dividends and receiving their monetary distribution when the corporation is liquidated. They get paid first, and common stock holders get what is left over. Sometimes, preferred stockholders do not have the right to vote. In addition, preferred stock can be transferred to common stock.

Hybrid stock is a stock entity that is not true equity stock. For example, a promissory note — a document establishing a loan — that promises to convert into shares of common stock is known as hybrid stock. The privileges and rights of each of a corporation's classes of stockholders must be specifically described in the articles of incorporation.

The distinction between authorized shares and outstanding shares must be understood in the context of share structure. Authorized shares refer to the amount of shares of a corporation's stock that the corporation's board of directors has the power to issue. This amount is described in the corporation's articles of incorporation. A corporation is not permitted to underwrite shares above the amount of authorized shares or the excess shares have no legal tender. Authorized shares are like blank checks — they have no value until after a vote of directors issues them to shareholders, at which point they become outstanding or issued shares.

Outstanding or issued shares are the number of shares that a corporation's board of directors has actually underwritten to shareholders. Once issued, they represent ownership in the company. When the directors vote to issue stock, one of the corporate officers will print the actual certificate with the date, number of shares involved, and the name of the shareholder. After the authorized shares have all been underwritten, the directors can no longer issue shares of stock until the articles of incorporation have been revised to increase the number of authorized shares. In some states, the number of authorized shares may affect the filing fee for the articles of incorporation — the more authorized shares to be written, the higher the filing fee. Keep this in mind when drafting your articles of incorporation to keep your fees low.

Authorized shares determine how many shares your corporation may underwrite and how much each will cost to potential stockholders. It varies from corporation to corporation. Some corporations authorize and underwrite just one share of stock to one stockholder, while others authorize and issue many more.

A corporation with high-growth expectations will authorize anywhere from 1 million to 1 billion shares of stock. A smaller corporation, however, will authorize between 1,000 and 1 million shares. A high amount of authorized stock ensures the price per share will be inexpensive. It is suggested that a single share of stock should not cost more than $2 per share initially, to raise money in the professional capital community during the early stages of a corporation's development.

Step 7: Write and file the articles of incorporation

As mentioned previously, the articles of incorporation must be written and filed with the secretary of state to establish your corporation as a legal entity. Normally a one-page document, the articles of incorporation include the following:

- Corporation's name
- Designated agent to receive legal papers for the corporation
- Number and type of authorized stock that the corporation is to issue

- Corporation's purpose
- Names of the initial directors (optional)
- Other optional matters, like the designation of specific type of corporation

You can view sample copies of articles of incorporation at the state's secretary of state Web site where you plan to incorporate. You can use them as guidelines to your own articles of incorporation. You should use each respective state's form articles of incorporation as a guideline when preparing your own.

Normally, you should not disclose the names of your directors unless it is required to do so, as in the state of Nevada. You can easily appoint directors after you file the articles of incorporation. As articles of incorporation are public documents, you should seek privacy for your directors and not include them initially. The same goes for the owners of the corporation. You should not disclose them publicly as to protect all parties from potential personal litigation.. As a private business, you are not required to disclose this information, and your directors and owners will be afforded more protection if the information is kept private. Many new business owners choose to incorporate in order to have this type of legal protection for the individuals involved.

For an additional fee, you can also expedite the processing of your articles of incorporation. Nevada offers one-day incorporation for $100. Delaware offers one-hour incorporation for $1,000, two-hour service for $500, same-day service for $100, and 24-hour service for $50. *A listing of all states' Web sites is provided in the Appendix.*

Step 8: Create your corporate kit and seal

Once you have filed your articles of incorporation, you should order your corporate kit and seal. Similar to the LLC kit, this is merely a loose-leaf binder that stores the articles of incorporation, bylaws, minutes of meetings, and a stock ledger. They cost between $50 and $100. As with the LLC kit, the corporate kit contains the following:

- Binder with the corporate name engraved on the spine on the book
- Sample bylaws and minutes of the organizational meeting
- Blank stock certificates
- Corporate seal
- Blank stock transfer ledger

Some corporate owners deem the corporate kit unnecessary, but getting the binder is a good idea, and the sample documents are available online. The kits often offer a sample S corporation selection, which can be inserted into the minutes. The corporate seal is a tool that embosses the seal of the corporation on documents. It contains the name of your corporation, state of incorporation, and date of incorporation. They are not demanded in every state anymore, but they come with the corporate kit. The stock certificates are the printed images of stock that are issued to shareholders. The stock ledger is simply the list of who owns how much stock in the corporation. It also charts sales, transfers, and other transactions of the shares of the corporation. The corporation's secretary usually maintains the stock ledger. You can purchase a corporate kit from corporation supply companies and other office supply stores.

Step 9: Name your corporation's directors

The directors are a corporation's elected managers, and the incorporator appoints the directors. Then, at annual meetings, shareholders vote on directors who will serve one-year terms. Directors are often re-elected at subsequent annual meetings. Corporations are required to have a minimum of one director.

First, decide how many directors you want for your corporation. Normally, you should select the number of directors in proportion to the number of shareholders you have. Nevada and Delaware allow one-director corporations and may be suitable for one or two shareholders. Conversely, California does not permit single-director corporations unless there is only one shareholder.

Shareholders of one-director corporations are more at risk. A concept known as alter-ego liability can harm shareholders who appear to have too much of a personal interest in the company and do not separate personal and corporate assets. A single director with unlimited authority may ignore important formalities if he or she goes unchecked. On the other hand, a board with more than one member reaches decisions through discussion, consensus, and vote.

The ideal minimum number of directors is three. Two directors are also appropriate for small corporations, but if there is a disagreement and the directors cannot come to a resolution, there may be a deadlock, which could end up in court. In addition, single-director corporations may not be able to attract capital. An odd number of directors will help ensure that there are no tie votes. Directors should always abstain from issues that result in a conflict of interest by avoiding votes where they have a vested interest. For example, if the corporation is planning on buying a property, and the director owns that property, he or she should not vote on that issue. If the corporation only has one director, however, he or she cannot abstain because without the director's vote, the corporation cannot take action.

In small corporations, shareholders are often both officers and directors. Consider the use of external directors who are neither shareholders nor regular employees. They can bring an objective view of things to the table, novel experience, and vast knowledge. Once you have made a decision regarding how many people will serve on the board of directors, select your directors. The incorporator is empowered with this responsibility because there are not yet any shareholders.

Remember, directors are accountable for mismanagement of corporations for which they are appointed. Courts acknowledge that in a pressurized business environment, directors must be given leeway to carry out their duties. Consequently, courts are hesitant to second-guess a director's management policies and adhere to the business judgment rule. This rule declares that courts will not reexamine business decisions or consider the directors liable for errors in judgment, as long as the directors were:

- Independent and unbiased
- Behaving in good faith
- Reasonably conscientious in keeping abreast of the facts

Some outside or external directors will not serve on the board if the corporation does not offer directors' and officers' liability insurance. This type of insurance shields a corporation's management from liability resulting from aggressive creditors or unhappy shareholders. This type of insurance can be very expensive for smaller corporations.

Step 10: Write your corporation's bylaws

The bylaws are the internal operating rules governing your corporation. They specify rules dealing with meetings, voting, quorums, elections, and the powers and responsibilities of directors and officers; bylaws can range from five to 20 pages. A corporate kit normally contains sample bylaws. Your corporation's bylaws should always be specific to your business, however, so you should use care when following someone else's samples. It is wise to use the sample bylaws as a guide to the format and structure, and to generate original content to fit that structure.

Bylaws, unlike articles of incorporation, are not filed with the state. Yet, you should keep them with your corporate books and records. The bylaws cover the following:

- Number of directors
- Powers and responsibilities of directors and officers
- Date and time of annual directors and shareholders meeting

- How to elect, appoint, and remove directors
- Requirements for quorum for shareholder votes
- Requirements for quorum for director votes
- How to vote by written consent, without showing up at a formal meeting
- How to give proxy to other shareholders

Once you have fully drafted your bylaws, they must be approved on behalf of the corporation. Since a board of directors has not yet been appointed, it falls on the incorporator to adopt the bylaws at the same time that he or she selects the directors. The incorporator will complete the form called Sample Action by Incorporator Appointing Directors and Approving Bylaws to make the directors and bylaws official.

Step 11: Call a directors' organizational meeting

One of the last steps to take before finalizing your incorporation is to have an organizational meeting of the board of directors. You must take minutes at this meeting. Because the agenda of the meeting is fairly standard with all new corporations, the minutes are prepared beforehand and followed at the meeting. The initial meeting is more of a formality to establish the corporation and its directors, rather than a meeting intended to actually accomplish any business-related goals.

The meeting is usually, but not necessarily, held at the corporation's office. A quorum of directors — a majority that is determined by each individual state — must appear, but all directors should still show. The organizational meeting covers the following issues, and the minutes should document the following matters:

- Date, time, place, and persons present at the meeting

- Who is chairman or woman; another must be secretary

- The date that the articles of incorporation were filed with the secretary of state

- Directors should waive formal notice of the meeting

- Confirmation of registered agent of corporation

- Approval of corporate seal and stock certificate form

- Appointment of corporation's principal office and officers

- Declaration of fiscal year

- Issuance of stock and declaration of amount and type of consideration paid for above

- Statement of integrity of stock, saying that no advertising was involved and that it was in compliance with federal and state securities laws

Step 12: Obtain an employer identification number

Because your newly created corporation is a full-fledged legal entity, you must obtain an employer identification number (EIN) as required by federal law. This number is also required to open up a bank account. Just complete Form SS-4, Application for Employer Identification Number, or apply online. The online procedure is relatively new and can save time and energy. When you mail the form, it usually takes approximately six weeks. By faxing, it will take approximately five days. You can obtain a number immediately by calling the IRS directly. This is only available in some states, and you may have to hold the line for a while.

Step 13: Maintain your corporation

Once you obtain your EIN, the incorporation of your business is complete. Now, you must observe corporate formalities and maintain your corporation with the secretary of state's office to remain in good standing. Once you have completed your paperwork, including filing and paying your fees, you will receive the limited liability protection that corporations in good standing receive. The next chapter will discuss how to operate and maintain your corporation in good standing.

Tax Considerations

Corporations pay out their profits primarily as salaries or dividends. An owner who works for the corporation as an officer or employee receives his or her payout as a salary. This salary gets deducted from the corporation's income because the IRS sees reasonable salary payouts to be an ordinary and essential business expense. The salary is thus only taxed once — at the owner-employee's individual income tax rate. Corporate owners not only receive salaries, but also receive payments in the form of dividends as shareholders. Passive owners only receive dividends, not salaries. Because dividends cannot be deducted from the corporation's income, these monies are taxed twice — once on the corporate level, as part of the corporation's income, and again on the individual level, as part of the shareholder's income.

On the other hand, many small corporations need to monetize business growth with earnings that are not distributed to investors. These corporations request their investors to be patient and put off a return on their investment until the corporation's value increases. Regular or C corporations demand two levels of tax reporting and payment. First, the corporation must remit income taxes on profits that are kept in the business. Second, owners who receive salaries or dividends on profits must pay individual income taxes on these amounts.

With pass-through taxation, all profits flow through the business and are reported and taxed at the owner's individual income tax rate on the individual's income tax return. This is true even when profits are left in the business and not distributed to individual owners as salaries. As your business makes more money, it gets added to the income you may make in addition to the business such as your spouse's income, independent contractor work, and any other salary you make at another job. All this income gets taxed at the highest individual rate. This can be painful. The more money that you make through pass-through taxation, the more taxes you will have to pay at the end of the year, even if you leave the profits in the business and do not draw from them.

Although this dual taxation may seem cumbersome, many businesses prefer corporate taxation to pass-through taxation because it ultimately can save taxes for corporate owners. Since corporations have a life of their own outside of the owners, profits left in a corporation are taxed only to the corporation at corporate income tax rates, not to the owners. Moreover, corporations can deduct profits distributed to owners who work in the business (such as employees/shareholders) to culminate in a taxable income. These salaries are taxable exclusively to the employee/shareholder at his or her taxable rate, not to the corporation. Due to this splitting of profits between the corporation and its owners, owners can spread business profits out across the lower corporate and individual tax brackets. This enables corporate owners to pay lower taxes on business profits. Take a look at the chart below for the 2009-2010 Federal Corporate Income Tax Rates:

Taxable Income Over	Not Over	Tax Rate
$0	$50,000	15%
$50,000	$75,000	25%
$75,000	$100,000	34%
$100,000	$335,000	39%
$335,000	$10,000,000	34%
$10,000,000	$15,000,000	35%
$15,000,000	$18,333,333	38%
$18,333,333	-----	35%

Tax rates according to **www.irs.gov**

For example, Harriet and Hy own and operate a hair salon. Each owner will net $50,000 at the end of the year. This extra income will be taxed to Harriet and Hy at a rate of 35 percent. If Harriet and Hy incorporated their business, they could keep some or all of their profits in their corporation, where it would be taxed at initial corporate income tax rates of 15 percent for the first $50,000 and 34 percent for the full $100,000. As these rates are lower than the 35 percent income tax rate on their respective individual tax returns, their tax bill would be considerably lower.

C corporations may retain up to $250,000 of profits without incurring the concern of the IRS. Certain types of personal service corporations are permitted smaller automatic retained earnings of $150,000. C corporations can keep profits higher than these amounts, as long as the owners have a legitimate reason for keeping money in the corporation and are not hiding profits in the corporation so they do not to pay out shareholders in the form of dividends. Let us take a look at the laws regarding tax treatment of corporate dividends. Federal law has diminished the income tax rate individuals must remit on corporate dividends to 15 percent — low-income taxpayers remit 5 percent. These monies are taxed separately from an individual's personal income. Previously, dividends were taxed at the top income tax rate of more than 15 percent.

A corporation is not allowed to deduct the monies it pays out to shareholders from its taxable income. This signifies that dividends are taxed twice — once to the corporation as its taxable income, and once to the shareholder at his or her taxable income. Changes to this federal law have been proposed that would allow corporations to deduct the dividends from their taxable income, leaving only the shareholder to pay tax, but this effort has not passed. Also, under federal tax law, corporations receive a break in their income tax on dividends they receive as shareholders. This means that corporations that hold shares in other corporations may leave out 70 to 100 percent of dividend income from their taxable income. That is why corporations often invest in the stock of other corporations.

Operating a Corporation

So now you are in business. You have filed your articles of incorporation, selected your directors, held your first annual meeting, obtained your EIN, and opened your bank account: You even have your corporate seal to make it official. In choosing this business entity, you were fully cognizant that it is the most highly regulated entity of all the business entities. So how do you go about running the corporation and complying with all the rules and regulations, while at the same time preserving the limited liability protection you sought in the first place?

As just noted, you might have chosen the corporation for the limited liability protection it provides to its owners. This protects your personal assets from creditors and lawsuits filed against your company. However, this protection for shareholders is not absolute. The concepts of alter-ego liability and piercing the corporate veil give courts the authority to ignore the corporate liability protection and levy liability on shareholders in obvious cases of shareholder misconduct or illegal activity such as theft or deceit. The concepts of alter-ego liability and piercing the corporate veil apply to both LLCs and corporations.

First, alter-ego liability (as its name infers) means that a company's owner or owners have treated the company indistinguishable from themselves. Without the owners treating the company as separate from themselves, they are liable for the company's obligations — both legally and financially. An example of alter ego liability is if owners make allocations of cash or property to themselves when their company faces liabilities from creditors. This would occur when a corporation purchases $50,000 of product on credit from Company X. The corporation then sells the product and allocates $100,000 of profit to themselves without paying back Company X. A court would likely decide that the corporation made a wrongful allocation, and Company X would get a judgment against the corporation.

Second, piercing the corporate veil occurs when a creditor asks the court to ignore the company liability shield to reach its owners. An example of piercing the corporate veil occurs when owners fail to properly identify the business in corporate correspondence, advertisements, and contracts. This can happen when an individual signs a letter or contract instead of signing on behalf of the company. This paves the way for the creditor to pierce the corporate veil and claim they thought they were dealing with an individual who then may become liable for legal and financial debt when the issue arises. Therefore, when operating a corporation or an LLC, it becomes important to maintain honesty and integrity to protect your liability shield.

A corporation, like an LLC, is deemed a foreign corporation in a state when it transacts business in a state other than its state of incorporation. States normally demand that foreign businesses transacting business within their state lines qualify and register as foreign corporations; this is qualification. There are several reasons why states require foreign corporations to register to do business in their state. First, they are paying for the favor of doing business there. After all, if you are a New York corporation doing business in Florida, you are competing with the other Florida corporations and LLCs, all of whom paid fees to do business there. Second, consumer protection becomes an issue.

Once you register your business to qualify to do business in a foreign state, you are subject to jurisdiction in that state. You appoint an agent there whose job is to accept legal documents, and you can be sued in that state. Thus, consumers in that state are protected from your corporation's misdeeds should there be any, and your corporation becomes accountable to them and others.

The process of qualifying to do business as a foreign corporation is similar to incorporating your business. You must submit your articles of incorporation in the foreign state in addition to a submission that includes state-specific information, such as the resident agent you have chosen to serve in that state. The fees for qualification are as much, and often more, to qualify in a foreign state. Once qualified to do business in a foreign state, a corporation must do the following in the foreign state:

- File periodic reports
- File tax returns and pay taxes
- Appoint a local agent

Therefore, be judicious when deciding whether to register and qualify to do business in a foreign state. Despite the fact that every state requires foreign corporations to register, few if no states make a significant effort to enforce the foreign qualification rules. To maintain your corporation in good standing, you must observe the following formalities:

- Notice annual and special meetings
- Hold annual meetings of shareholders and annual meetings of directors
- Draft minutes of all meetings

- Meet quorum requirements for voting

- Hold a vote to remove directors and officers

- Observe conflicts of interest for directors and share-holders when conducting transactions and entering contracts

Annual meetings

The stockholders' most important duty is to select the corporate directors. This is accomplished at the share-holders' annual meeting. The bylaws usually set forth the date, time, and place of the meeting. Sometimes the meeting is held after the end of the fiscal year when shareholders can discuss the financial performance of the corporation. Because the date of the annual meeting is described in the bylaws, notice for this particular meeting is not required. Nonetheless, it is a good idea to remind shareholders of the meeting. The annual meeting of the directors can be held simultaneously.

To hold a lawful shareholder vote, a quorum of shareholders must be in existence. Quorum rules stop a small minority of shareholders from controlling the corporation. Remember, some corporations have different classes of shareholders, and not all necessarily have voting rights. In addition, in terms of these meetings, the directors will select a record date, which establishes when an individual must own shares to receive the benefits of ownership, such as voting rights. This record date becomes an important piece of information because in publicly traded companies, shares often are traded from one individual to another. State law stipulates that a majority of the outstanding voting shares establishes a quorum, but corporate organizers can lower the number of shares that establishes a quorum by adding a specific provision to the bylaws stipulating a different amount. Remember that the minimum number for a quorum differs from state to state. Nonetheless, for smaller corporations, the quorum should be created at a simple majority: 51 percent.

From time to time, special meetings of shareholders may be held. These are meetings held in addition to a periodic meeting described in the bylaws, for example the annual meeting. Special shareholder meetings are often held to make changes to the board of directors. This entails removing the entire board, removing some of the directors, or taking care of a vacancy. The rules that govern calling a special meeting are:

- The shareholder(s) that notice the meeting must own a minimum percentage of a corporation's outstanding shares — usually about 5 or 10 percent.

- Officers and directors also have the right to call special shareholder meetings.

- The individual who calls for the meeting in a written document must submit the document to the corporate secretary, who must then notice the meeting.

- Notice must be distributed to all shareholders indicating the time and place of the meeting and what is to be discussed.

In a corporation, voting by proxy is when one shareholder gives another shareholder the authority to vote his or her shares. Proxy is also the name for the written tool that confers such authority. Rules for proxy are normally included in the state law and a corporation's bylaws. Proxies can declare the period of time for which they can be utilized. If no time span is mentioned, the proxy will lapse automatically by state law. For example, a proxy that fails to declare a duration remains usable for eleven months in California and three years in Delaware. A proxy may either grant the proxy holder absolute power to vote the shares as they desire, or a long-form proxy may declare the specific issues for which the proxy was granted in the first place. Some states require larger corporations to utilize long-form proxies.

All annual and special meetings must be recorded. These written recordings of the activities taken at such meetings are called minutes. Minutes are easy to draft and are often short. As a guideline, minutes of meetings should always include:

- The type of meeting (shareholders, annual, board of directors)

- Whether the meeting was called by notice or a written waiver of notice

- Attendance

- Actions taken at the meeting (filling a vacancy, removing an officer, real estate purchase)

- Signature of the individual taking the minutes of the meeting, usually the secretary

Written consent authorizes shareholders and directors to take an action without a meeting. A written consent is simply an official written tool that describes a corporate action to be taken, and it is executed by the shareholders and directors agreeing to the action. Many directors and managers find written consents easier and more convenient than noticing meetings. Actions taken by consent do not require minutes to be recorded as the written consent memorializes the action. For some corporate events, such as the election of directors or the revision of the articles of incorporation, written consents must be unilateral. A written consent includes the following:

- Type of action taken (director's or shareholder's action)

- Declaration stating that the shareholders or directors have taken the action rescind notice of a meeting

- Actions taken (election of directors, issuance of stock, amendment of bylaws)

- Signature of director or shareholder who has voted on the action

Every corporation's directors should meet once a year whether ordered by law or not. The date for such a meeting is usually described in the corporation's bylaws. Normally, it succeeds the annual meeting of shareholders. At the annual meeting, directors select officers who serve a year until the next annual meeting. Other corporate actions taken by the directors may also occur at the annual meeting. Although it is not required because it is set forth in the bylaws, directors should still send out reminders of the annual meeting. Special meetings of shareholders and special meetings of directors can be held at any time. Because the duties of directors are so manifold, these meetings can be called for any purpose.

As with the LLC's membership ledger, an important record of your corporation is known as the share ledger. The share ledger, also known as the share transfer ledger or share registry, is a document stating each shareholder's name, the number of shares he or she has, and the disposition of the shares. All new corporations should create a share ledger, and update it when shares are sold, gifted, transferred, or when new shares are written. All shares in a corporation are regulated by comprehensive state and federal limitations on sale and transfer unless such shares are registered. Registered shares simply mean publicly traded shares that are sold in public markets like the stock exchange. Therefore, if you sell shares in a company that is not public, you must make sure you follow the exemptions permitted by state and federal law.

Remember, almost all states demand corporations to submit periodic reports with the secretary of state's office or other official department. A corporation submits its periodic report in the state in which it is incorporated and the state in which it is qualified to do business as a foreign corporation. California and Alaska only require corporations to submit periodic reports every two years. The fees, due dates, and late penalties differ from state to state. Some states such as California, Georgia, and Arkansas permit filing of periodic reports online. Check your state's secretary of state Web site to determine whether you can exercise this option. *A list of the state Web sites is provided in the Appendix.*

Shareholders may want to amend the corporation's articles of incorporation. How do they do this? They vote either at an annual meeting of shareholders or at a special meeting. Conversely, they may do so by written consent. Any proposed amendment to the articles of incorporation must be submitted to the secretary of state. It does not take effect legally until the secretary of state approves the submission. Some states demand either a supermajority vote or a unanimous vote to accept the proposal. The secretary of state mainly cares about whether the amendment changes the rights of existing shareholders insofar as amendments authorizing additional shares would diminish the value of those of existing shareholders. Typical amendments to articles of incorporation are changing the name of the corporation, increasing the number of authorized shares, and adopting an additional class of shares.

Normally, both shareholders and directors have the privilege to amend bylaws. Some states, but not all, execute partial limitations on the rights of directors to revise bylaws. A corporation's bylaws will outline the procedure for how to amend the bylaws. Unlike amendments to articles of incorporation, amendments to bylaws do not have to be filed with the state because they are not legal documents. These amendments take effect immediately upon approval by either the board of directors or shareholders. Typical amendments to bylaws include increasing or decreasing the number of directors and changing the date for the corporation's annual meeting.

Corporations are separate legal entities and exist in perpetuity until they are dissolved. *Dissolution of a business is discussed in more detail in Chapter 9.* Essentially, dissolution is the procedure of ending the life of a corporation by settling its accounts with creditors, allocating its net assets to its shareholders, and shutting it down for business. There are three types of dissolution:

Voluntary dissolution is voted on by the directors at a board of directors meeting or by written consent. Then, the director files a notice of dissolution or application for dissolution with the secretary of state. Sometimes, the secretary of state will not accept the voluntary dissolution of a corporation if it is not in good standing or has tax liabilities. Ironically, the next step for such a corporation would be administrative dissolution when a government agency steps in.

The secretary of state has the authority to order an **administrative dissolution** of the corporation. They can exercise that power when the corporation does not fulfill its statutory obligations such as periodic filings and reporting of taxes. The standards for an administrative dissolution vary from state to state. Some states permit a reinstatement after the proper filings have been recorded following an administrative dissolution.

A **judicial dissolution** acts upon the request of the attorney general, shareholder, or creditor. For example, a shareholder may bring a legal action to dissolve a corporation if he or she feels that the corporation is wasting assets, if his or her rights are being trampled on by other shareholders, or if the voting between shareholders and directors has deadlocked.

As a business owner, director, or shareholder, you should try to avoid dissolution at all costs. This can lead to a breakdown in the corporation's liability protection. Even when voluntarily dissolving, you should be careful. Do not dissolve a corporation when in debt. If you dissolve a corporation as a shareholder, and the corporation has debts or liabilities, they may be passed on to you.

Advantages and disadvantages

The advantages of the corporation are many. Owners are protected from personal liability in the form of legal judgments and business debts. That is, creditors may not seize your personal assets, such as a bank account, car, home, boat, or anything else, in satisfaction of a bad debt or legal judgment the corporation makes — only the corporation is liable. Also, corporations have a legal framework from which to operate. State laws govern the corporation and provide rules for operation and management.

Corporations are the best mode for eventual public companies when shares of stock can be sold for public ownership of the company. A major advantage of corporations is that they can raise capital, not only through the initial public offering (IPO); also, banks and lending institutions grant loans to corporations faster than sole proprietorships and partnerships. Ownership can easily be transferred through the sale of stock. Corporations exist "in perpetuity," so they live outside of the owner and shareholder. That means when the owner dies, the corporation still exists. An important advantage of corporations is that they can provide tax benefits with its double taxation by putting an amount that would otherwise be subject to high rates on an individual personal tax return, into a corporate account that may be taxed less.

There are also several disadvantages of corporations. They are highly regulated and have required annual meetings, and owners and directors must follow certain formalities. They cost more to set up than partnerships and sole proprietorships. And, they must file periodically with the government and pay annual fees.

CASE STUDY: FORMING AN S CORPORATION

Eduardo and Lydia Dia
Diamond Care Villas
20316 Lanark St.
Winnetka, CA 91306
Phone: 818-739-9008

We have been in this business for almost two years now. It is a home-care facility for the elderly with two direct care staff and one administrator. The most common — and most serious —mistake people make in business is not picking the right type of business to begin with. Before I entered into this business, I considered the following issues to avoid pitfalls: (a) Do I really want to be in the business? (b) What type of business do I really want to be in and where? Location is very important; (c) Can I work full-time, or afford not to?

After considering all these factors, I chose to form an S corporation and be a health care provider for the elderly. We picked the name Diamond Care Villa, mainly because the first three letters of the word "diamond" are the same as my last name: Dia. Also, a diamond is a precious gem, so we can translate that to mean our business as a perfect, unharmed, and flawless way of giving care to the elderly. We always treat our customers with dignity and great respect.

I found my lawyer through a friend who has been in this business for number of years already. Yes, I recommend using a lawyer because he or she can effectively assert and protect the interest of the business as well as the owners. These experienced lawyers can handle all complex matters. So, I strongly suggest hiring a legal consultant.

In our business, the most difficult thing we experienced when we started was the marketing side. I did not expect the competition to be stiff in our area because of the number of facilities available. So, we decided to practice door-to-door solicitation. We focused our market solicitation in all the hospitals, retirement hotels, rehabilitation centers, and convalescent hospitals around and outside our area. We mostly depend on word-of-mouth from referrals.

We got our capital through our savings in the bank, and we also opened a business line of credit to finance big expenditures that our business encountered through the course of operations. Conservatively speaking, I expected a profit after two years. Currently, we are breakeven due to continuous increases in prices of all commodities while our income remains the same. The company has liability insurance that protects the company from any legal problems.

Some benefits of my business formation as an S corporation include the following:

- It has limited liability, meaning all debts incurred by the corporation are the responsibility of the corporation and not by shareholders who can only be held accountable up to the amount of our investment.

- We can avoid double taxation legally from the IRS. All of the corporation's profits are considered to be our income. We are required to file personal federal tax returns but not to pay a federal corporate tax.

- All losses can be deducted on my personal return.

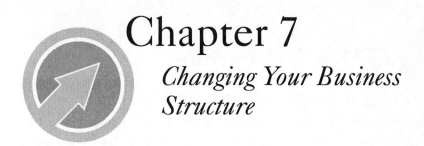

Chapter 7

Changing Your Business Structure

Determining the Right Time for a Change

You may have started your business at a time when you wanted to work alone or were uncertain as to the chances for success you would have with your new venture. In this case, you probably decided to run your business as a sole proprietor. As your business grew, you brought on an employee or two and decided you needed a little extra protection (and maybe even some tax breaks) for you and your business. At this point, you may want to investigate the options for converting your sole proprietorship into an LLC or even a corporation.

In the other direction, you may have started out too big and now need to downgrade. You had big dreams and wanted your business to be seen as a corporation, for the image or for increased financing potential. Now, after reviewing your liability potential and the need to maintain paperwork, you realize that you will be better served in a less formal entity, such as an LLC or a sole proprietorship. Whatever the case, if you have decided it is now time for a change, the following will help you determine the pros and cons of changing your structure, as well as give guidance as to the steps to follow.

Changing Your Tax Structure

Now that you know the tax structures of each business entity, you will be able to make an intelligent decision regarding which entity you wish to use. If you have already selected a business entity, you are better informed about whether you want to convert it to another. Alternatively, if you are perfectly content with the business entity you have, you may want to change your tax classification, from pass-through to corporate or corporate to pass-through. This section will discuss how you can change your classification with new federal tax law legislation. This principle is known as "entity classification election" or "special election." It allows a partnership to be taxed like a corporation or allows corporation owners to choose pass-through tax treatment.

You should know that you may be able to transfer to a more favorable tax situation when your business structure changes, and you may not necessarily be restricted to a default tax classification. Nevertheless, it is normally best to choose a business structure with a default tax classification that will work for you from the get-go. Changing your tax classification will have long-term disadvantages. For example, after you change your tax classification, the IRS will demand that you wait five years before changing your classification again. As discussed before, frequent changes tend to arouse suspicions regarding the business owner's motives. There are some exceptions to this rule, but they might not be applicable to your business. You should consult a tax adviser before changing your tax status.

Unincorporated business structures such as LLCs and partnerships have the capability to change from pass-through to corporate tax treatment. It is simply a matter of checking the correct box on IRS Form 8832 Entity Classification Election. After you submit this form, your unincorporated business will get the same treatment as a corporation — without the hassle and expense of establishing a corporation — under the Internal Revenue Code for all purposes, including employee fringe benefits, income tax reporting and paying, stock option plans, and sale and redemption of the business's interests.

After the change of business structure is processed, the unincorporated business files corporate tax returns and then has the right to split business income between the business — which will pay corporate income taxes on monies kept in the business — and the individual owners, who now pay individual income taxes on salaries paid to them as employees of the corporation. The corporate salaries owners receive for services rendered while running the corporation may be deducted from the corporation's taxable income. Direct distribution of corporate profits to owners will be treated as corporate dividends and taxed accordingly. Moreover, if an owner sells his or her corporate share in the business in the future, the IRS will treat that transaction as a sale of corporate stock and tax it. Take a look at the following example:

Clean Kitchens LLC installs and creates kitchen cabinets. The company is owned by a married couple named Bobbie and Doug. Business is booming, and profits are soaring. Bobbie and Doug have put most of the profits back into the business for inventory and improvements. Bobbie and Doug do not want to pay taxes on the money put back into the business on their individual tax returns. They question whether they should incorporate their business so they will only have to pay the lower corporate tax rates on these monies. If Bobbie and Doug submit IRS Form 8832 to select a corporate tax status, their business still remains an LLC under state law, but is taxed as a corporation under federal law. Note that most states will also consider the business as a corporation for state income tax purposes once the choice is made on the federal form. This tax selection permits them to split income between themselves and the LLC, diluting it between the lower corporate and individual income tax brackets, instead of having it all taxed at the higher individual rates.

The result is that the money kept in the LLC is taxed at the lower 15 percent and 25 percent corporate income tax rates. The monies paid to Bobbie and Doug in return for services rendered is now considered corporate salary, which is subtracted from the LLC's income and taxed only to Bobbie and Doug on their joint individual income tax return. Because they elected corporate tax treatment, Bobbie and Doug's sum total LLC and individual taxes on profits are less than they would have been had they chosen pass-through tax status and reported the profits on their tax return and paid individual rates.

Can sole proprietorships also change their tax status? The privilege of changing tax classifications belongs solely to "business entities," and since the sole proprietorship is not a business entity under the federal tax regime because it does not exist apart from its owner, it cannot. It does not have the option of filing IRS Form 8832 as an LLC or partnership does. If you are a sole proprietor and want to change your tax options, consult your financial adviser.

Corporations have the capability to change their tax classification from corporate to pass-through treatment. Yet, corporations cannot directly adapt the tax classification of a sole proprietorship or partnership. Instead, the Internal Revenue Code (and similar provisions in most states' tax laws) establishes a special form of pass-through tax treatment for corporations under Subchapter S of Title 26 of the Internal Revenue Code, Tax Treatment of S Corporations and Their Shareholders. This entity provides pass-through tax treatment.

Changing a Partnership to an LLC

Often, partnerships like to change business formations into an LLC. Normally, the partners who do this are seeking the limited liability protection for their personal assets. Once this is accomplished, all the general partners attain limited liability protection after the LLC is created. If you are talking about a limited partnership being changed to an LLC, not only do the limited partners maintain their limited liability protection, but they can assume management positions in the LLC. In most states, a general partnership can convert to an LLC with a small amount of paperwork and fees, and with no difference in income tax treatment. We will now examine the legal processes necessary for converting a general or limited partnership to an LLC. To convert a general partnership to an LLC, the partners must consent to ending the partnership and change to an LLC by following these steps:

1. **Consult your partnership agreement.** Most partnership agreements need the unanimous agreement of all owners or partners to alter the form of the business. Even if it is not so stipulated in the agreement, you should have everyone in agreement before changing to an LLC, or any other business formation, for that matter. This may require more paperwork to legally terminate your partnership. Then, you may have to publish a notice of dissolution in your local newspaper to inform creditors and all interested parties. This is handled with a modest fee. Call your newspaper to determine whether this is required in your state, and how you go about doing it, if required.

2. **File the appropriate paperwork.** The owners must file LLC articles of incorporation with the state filing office, normally the corporations department of the secretary of state. Some states offer a form online specifically for this purpose. Check your secretary of state's Web site. Let us look at an example of how to convert a partnership to an LLC: Irving and Molly are partners in a catering business. They want to convert to an LLC. Each one owns 50 percent. They have a computer and go to the secretary of state's corporation's Web site and find a standard articles of organization form — not a specific articles of conversion form. They download the form, and both sign together to show they agree to the conversion. They mail it in to-

gether with the required fees to the secretary of state's office. Irving then calls the local newspaper to place a notice of dissolution partnership notice. The newspaper then informs them that yes, it is required, and yes, they can publish it. After paying for three weeks of publication — separated by a week in between each — the newspaper sends Irving an affidavit of publication showing copies of the notice of dissolution in the newspaper. Irving pastes the clippings in the LLC records book and the conversion is complete.

3. **Draft your operating agreement.** The new owners should prepare an operating agreement for the newly formed LLC. The LLC's operating agreement is similar to the partnership agreement in that it governs and documents the business entity. The operating agreement contains ownership interests, profits, losses, voting and liquidation rights, and the other duties and entitlements of the LLCs members. The operating agreement also specifies how the LLC is to be managed — either by its members (member-management) or by a specific management team (manager-management team composed of members and non-members). Normally in a partnership to LLC conversion, member-management is implemented, as it most closely resembles the management structure of the partnership. In addition, the capital, profits, and voting interests of the partners may be replicated from the partnership agreement to the operating agreement. Even though LLCs are normally treated like partnerships under state and federal law, you may not be able to carry over all of

the provisions because there are some differences in tax treatment. Consult a tax attorney before doing your final draft of the operating agreement.

4. **Secure updated permits, licenses, and registrations.** The new LLC should get new permits, licenses, and registrations in the name of the LLC, and it should rescind old licenses and permits that exist in the name of the old partnership. If the LLC is going to operate under a different name than the name specified in its articles of organization, it should file a DBA with the county clerk.

5. **You should also obtain an EIN.** If the old partnership had an EIN, it is not necessary to get a new one; you can use the old number. If you co-own a new LLC and have no employees or retirement plan, you still have to get a number for your new LLC. In any case, the LLC needs an EIN to prepare its annual IRS and state information returns.

To convert a limited partnership to an LLC, the owners/ partners must consent to a conversion to an LLC. Though, unlike a general partnership, a limited partnership must officially dissolve by filing paperwork with the state agency that handles such matters — normally the corporations division of the secretary of state's office. Often, the state utilizes the articles of conversion form. If your state does not provide this form, you can file a certificate of cancellation of limited partnership. Whichever form you file, it may still be necessary to publish a notice of dissolution of limited partnership in a local county newspaper where your partnership was located. Call your local newspaper to find out whether this procedure is necessary for your state. Follow these steps to convert a limited partnership to an LLC:

1. **File the articles of organization.** It is required that the owners of the limited partnership file LLC articles of organization with the state. Several states offer an online copy that you can download for your convenience. If you use the special articles of conversion form to convert your limited partnership to an LLC, you do not have to also file a certificate of cancellation of limited partnership.

   Let us look again at the example of Irving and Molly and their catering business. They have a limited partnership and want to convert to an LLC. The state does not offer the special articles of conversion of partnership to LLC form. Thus, Irving completes and files standard articles of organization as he did in the previous example. He then locates and downloads a certificate of cancellation of limited partnership and dates it when he filed the articles of organization. If he had located the articles of conversion of partnership to LLC form, he would have been able to accomplish two things at once — the creation of the LLC and the dissolution of his partnership. He would not have had to file the certificate of cancellation of limited partnership and the articles of organization. But this form was not available, so he had to file the two forms in a two-step process.

2. **Draft your operating agreement.** The new owners should prepare an LLC operating agreement describing ownership interests, profits, losses, voting and

liquidation rights, and the other duties and entitlements of the members. Normally, the new LLC is manager-management structured, with the former general partner acting as the new manager-member of the LLC. The previous limited partners become non-managing members. Thus the new LLC replicates the old limited partnership in its structure. Similar to general partnerships, most clauses of the partnership agreement (regarding capital, profits, and voting interests) may be carried over to the new operating agreement, with the exception of clauses having to do with special allocations and tax treatment, which should be looked over by a tax attorney.

3. **Update licenses, permits, and registrations.** Just as in a general partnership, once your limited partnership becomes an LLC, you should obtain new licenses, permits, and registrations in the new business's name, and cancel any permits, licenses, and registrations in the old business's name. If you will do business under a name different from the name in your articles of organization, file a DBA with the county clerk's office.

4. **Secure an EIN.** You may continue to use the same employer identification number as the old limited partnership.

Converting a Partnership to a Corporation

Before LLCs, partnerships had no choice but to convert to LLCs to obtain limited liability protection. Now, with the advent of LLCs, partnerships have a choice between LLCs and corporations if they seek limited liability protection. Most partnerships will convert to LLCs if they want limited liability protection and pass-through tax status. Nevertheless, there are still many reasons for partnerships to convert to corporations.

Attaining more sources of capital is the biggest reason why many partnerships incorporate. Venture capital companies normally only fund corporations because only that entity meets their needs for special management, dividends, liquidation, and voting rights that are intrinsic to classes of corporate stock. Savvy investors and venture fund managers realize that investing in a corporation offers the best means of securing liquid assets so they can obtain the cash they put in when they want to withdraw from the company.

For example: Gary and Paula, programmers and business partners, have invented a new video game. Ira and Judy are owners of a venture capital firm called Our Money is Your Money LLC. The four want to fund a start-up company, specifically a corporation, to develop and license the game. Ira and Judy agree to pay rent for office space and hire a software management and development team to create a prototype that they can pitch to video game companies. In exchange for that monetary support, Gary and Paula will transfer their partnership assets relating to the video game (the code and their rights to the software) to the new corporation in exchange for stock. Our Money is Your Money will be 52 percent common shareholder, and Gary and Paula will each be 24 percent common shareholders. Our Money is Your Money will also receive 10 percent of the total number of common shares in nonvoting preferred shares that have a special right to dividends (assuming earnings and profits reach a certain number). Moreover, Our Money is Your Money will be assured a return of five times the original value of the preferred shares before any sales proceeds are paid out on the common shares. One of the original partners, Gary or Paula, will serve on the three-person board of directors with Ira and Judy, so Ira and Judy will maintain a majority on the board and control the corporation.

So, not only are Gary and Paula receiving funding for a new office and development team, but they are also promised part ownership in the new company. They may not have had the means to develop their idea any further than the conception stage without striking a deal with the venture capital firm and agreeing to liquidate their partnership assets. Of course, Gary and Paula should check with their legal advisers to determine if the numbers verify how lucrative a deal it really is.

Cumulative voting is another reason why partnerships choose to form a corporation rather than an LLC. Cumulative voting occurs when minority shareholders in a corporation attain more power when electing shareholders to the board of directors. Let us look at an example:

Consider Paula and Gary, again. They have agreed to form a corporation with the money from Our Money is Your Money, which will be a 52 percent common shareholder, and Paula and Gary will be each be 24 percent common shareholders. According to standard corporate shareholder voting rules, each shareholder can vote on issues presented to shareholders. Our Money is Your Money holds a majority at 52 shares and can vote all 52 shares for each candidate to the board. It can thus theoretically decide who will hold each of the three seats. Nonetheless, under cumulative voting, each board member acquires total votes equivalent to his or her shares, multiplied by the number of directors to be elected. Under this calculation, Our Money is Your Money would get a total of 156 votes (52x3), while Gary and Paula will have 72 votes each (24x3), for a total of 144 votes. To make a long story short, strategically pooling their votes under cumulative voting assures the minority shareholders, Gary and Paula, have sufficient votes to elect their directorial candidate to a position on the board as the third candidate.

Partnerships should choose to convert to corporations rather than LLCs for other additional reasons. One reason would be tax splitting and corporate income. If your business is doing well, and you want to keep the money in the business instead of taking it out, corporate income tax rates are lower than individual income tax rates for the saved amount. It thus makes sense to incorporate so you can split your income and not get the high top income tax rates of the individual business owner.

Another reason to convert would be equity-based employee plans. If owners want to attract the best and the brightest employees to their company, they might want to offer stock option plans where employees can earn or buy part ownership in the company. This option is not available to LLCs. A third reason to convert would be to enjoy the benefits of the corporate structure. For a partnership seeking to grow and attain a managerial structure, the corporation offers a built-in structure through its directors, officers, and share-holders positions, each with distinct rights and responsi-bilities. Finally, there are tax-free perks to converting to a corporation. Tax-free benefits such as medical reimburse-ment plans and tax-free premiums paid for up to $50,000 worth of qualified term-life insurance are available to your employees if you own a corporation and to you as an em-ployee of your own corporation. You automatically become an employee of your business when you incorporate.

There are other tax advantages to forming a corporation rather than an LLC that are beyond the scope of this book, but it is best to say that corporations become the attractive business entity to the entrepreneur who wants to grow his or her business or sees himself or herself being acquired by a larger business. If you wish to start on a smaller scale and do not have your sights set as high, an LLC would probably be a better choice. You can always convert your LLC to a corporation once it grows. Note that converting a sole proprietorship, partnership, and LLC to a corpora-tion is a simpler, tax-free event, rather than the other way around. Converting a corporation to a sole proprietorship, partnership, or LLC involves the dissolution of the entity for both legal and tax purposes, whereby both the corpora-tion and its shareholders may owe income taxes.

From a general partnership to a corporation

The legal procedures for converting a general partnership to a corporation begin with securing the consent of the owners to end the partnership and change to a corpora-tion. Most partnership agreements contain provisions that require the unanimous consent of all partners to dissolve or create a different business entity. Even if it is not included in the partnership agreement, it is advisable to obtain the written consent of all partners before you proceed. After all, each partner's tax and legal status changes with the change to a corporation, so it makes sense that each partner approves the plan to convert. Your state may demand that you publish a notice of dissolution of partnership in the local newspaper, so call your local newspaper to determine whether this is indeed required, how much it costs, and how you can go about it.

You will then file the articles of incorporation. Just as you would if you formed a corporation from the start, you must file articles of incorporation with the secretary of state's office when you convert your partnership to a corporation. Uniform forms are available online—check your state's secretary of state Web site, under "corporations division." You must pay a fee based on the number and type of shares established by the articles. Several states permit you to terminate a general or limited partnership and convert it to a corporation using simple articles of conversion form. If your state does not offer one, you can transfer your partnership to a corporation by making the aforementioned filing to dissolve your partnership, filing your articles of incorporation, and transferring the assets and liabilities of the old partnership to your corporation with a bill of sale. Remember, check with your tax advisor for any extenuating tax consequences to this conversion.

Next you will need to issue shares after transferring the assets and liabilities. Normally, the ex-partners distribute the liabilities and assets of the old partnership to the new corporation and receive shares of stock instead of cash. Partners normally receive a percentage of shares of stock in the new corporation that reflects their ownership interest in the old partnership. When any new owners or investors enter the fray, the must pay in cash or property for their shares of stock.

From a limited partnership to a corporation

To convert a limited partnership to a corporation, you must first dissolve the old partnership with a form called a Certificate of Cancellation of Limited Partnership, which must be executed by all parties. Obtain this form on the Internet at your state's corporate filing office Web site.

Additionally, some states permit a limited or general partnership (or LLC) to change to a corporation by simply filling out special articles of conversion. This is not a requirement, but it makes the conversion process a bit simpler. The form may be available on the secretary of state's corporation's Web site, or an attorney can prepare it. When you prepare and file this form, no other form is necessary to end the old partnership and create a corporation — it is a one-step legal process. Moreover, once this form is filed, the old partnership's assets and liabilities are automatically transferred to the new corporation, and no bill of sale is needed.

Another matter to be taken into consideration is to inform your old partnership's creditors of your new incorporated business. A friendly letter to your creditors will inform them that the new business will assume the old business's debts. Then, your new corporation cannot be held liable to creditors who continue to extend new credit to the business unbeknownst to your new status.

Converting a Sole Proprietorship or Partnership to an LLC

Suppose you are enjoying the pass-through taxation of a sole proprietorship or partnership, but you are starting to worry about losing your personal assets to creditors. Should you change your business structure to an LLC? Unless you are a small business with no debts or liabilities, or you already formed a corporation, the answer is yes. Why? Creating an LLC is extremely simple and pain-free. You just have to complete a standard form given by most state LCC-filing offices and file the form for a small fee. And what do you get for that small filing fee? Peace of mind from knowing your personal assets are protected from debts and liabilities arising from the course of business while, at the same time, enjoying the same pass-through tax status.

Sole proprietorships can easily be converted into LLCs, which may be the better option for your business. Suppose you want to open a retail store selling musical instruments. Customer traffic could result in a slip-and-fall lawsuit. You could also enter into contract disputes with suppliers of your product. In addition, customers might not be happy with their purchase; this would be a perfect candidate for an LLC business. For the fee of $125 to file the articles of organization with the state, and an additional $50 annual report fee, you could have limited liability protection from costly lawsuits. And because it is an LLC and not a corporation, you will not have to change your tax status from a sole proprietor. It can be seen that changing your business from a sole proprietorship to an LLC is an easy transition and protects you in the long run.

Partnerships can also be converted to LLCs. Suppose you and your partner operate a pet grooming business. Business is going well from your rented shop in the mall, but one of your customers threatens to sue because he said you made a cut in his dog's skin while grooming him. Now is the time to act. By filling out a one-page "Conversion of Partnership to an LLC" form provided by the state, you can convert your partnership to an LLC. The filing fee is minimal, and you and your partner both file taxes the same way you did in your partnership — individually on your personal tax return. To file taxes, the business must file IRS Form 1065, U.S. Return on Partnership Income. Thereafter, you can rest easy that your personal assets are protected from lawsuits. Nevertheless, your business assets are still vulnerable, so you must be careful how you proceed; it should be noted that not all states offer this form for partnership conversion. If your state does not, you and your partner should file standard articles of organization to form your LLC. Moreover, in some states, you must publish a newspaper ad to inform the public that you are ending your partnership relationship.

Converting a Sole Proprietorship to a Partnership

When you want to change owners of a sole proprietorship — for example, you wish to take on a partner — you must convert the sole proprietorship. This is a very common event, as most entrepreneurs start small businesses as sole proprietorships, and it occurs when the sole owner of a business brings in another owner. When you take on a second owner, you might consider an LLC as another option. The LLC affords limited liability protection. This is advisable, as bringing in a second partner subjects you to the possibility of liability for his or her business decisions and contracts.

Legal procedures

A one-person business automatically evolves into a general partnership once a second owner is brought into the fold. It is not necessary to file any additional paperwork with the state to implement this change. Once you have added another owner, you have created a partnership. Nevertheless, the partners in the new business should do the following things to get organized:

1. **Prepare a partnership agreement.** Partners should draft and execute a partnership agreement to corroborate how they have agreed to share ownership interests, losses, profits, and voting and liquidation rights, as well as to describe the rights and duties of the partners.

2. **Revise licenses, permits, and registrations.** The partners may need to update and edit government paperwork in the name of the new partnership. This could mean professional, state, and local licenses; state sales and use tax permits; and government reg-

istrations. Cancel any old licenses and other papers in the sole proprietorship's name. If the partnership will transact business under a new name that is different from the surnames of the partners, it must submit a new DBA request.

3. **Get an EIN.** The partnership should get a new employer identification number, even if there are no employees involved. Even when a partner shares in the profits, he or she is not considered an employee. The EIN is used on tax returns.

Tax consequences of conversion

The good news is that there are no direct income tax consequences when a sole proprietorship transitions into a partnership. The sole proprietor gives the assets of his or her business to the new partnership. According to Section 721(a) of the Internal Revenue Code, this is not a taxable situation: It is known as a "tax-neutral" change instead of a taxable sale or exchange under state and federal tax laws.

Nevertheless, in some events, the conversion may initiate taxation. When a partnership transfers a capital interest to a partner in exchange for the past or future services rendered, it may be a taxable situation. A capital interest means an investment in the partnership's assets that is paid later to the owner if he or she removes himself or herself from the partnership or when the partnership dissolves. If a capital interest is given for past or future services, the value of the interest will automatically be taxed as service income. The government taxes the partner performing the service as though the partnership had paid him in the present, rather than in the future. Look at the following example:

Ginger owns a successful sole proprietorship but wants a partner to help manage the business. She asks Laura to join her as an equal partner in exchange for entering in a ten-year, full-time employment contract. Laura hires an independent contractor to value the business, who values her half-interest at $150,000. To avoid having to pay taxes on $150,000, Laura decides to buy her half outright for some cash and a promissory note from Ginger to pay the partnership the remaining balance. Laura then enters into a separate employment contract with the partnership, which is not connected to her purchase of half of the company.

Because of this tax exception for capital interests, a partner who will render services to a partnership either:

- Elects to take a share of the earnings and profits of the partnership, which is not taxed in lieu of a capital interest.

- Buys the interest under other terms, such as for cash, property, or a promissory note, not for services rendered (such as the above example).

Procedures for tax filing

Once a sole proprietorship is converted to a partnership, the owners must submit IRS Form 1065, U.S. Return of Partnership Income, at the end of the tax year. The partnership must also complete a Schedule K-1 (Form 1065) Partner's

Share of Income, Credits, and Deductions to distribute to each partner. This form documents the amount of income or loss, deductions, credits, and other information each partner must submit on his or her individual 1040 tax return. Basically, the income tax treatment of profits earned in the business remains the same. That is, partners, like sole proprietors, report and pay income tax on all profits accumulated annually in the business, whether the company pays out profits to the partners or not. For payroll tax purposes, partners are not considered employees: They are owners.

Changing a Sole Proprietorship to an LLC

It is possible in most states for a sole proprietor to convert to an LLC with a minimum amount of paperwork and fees, and with no difference to the owner's income tax treatment and filing requirements. Nevertheless, there are exceptions to every rule, which can affect a sole proprietor's conversion to an LLC. For example, what occurs if one or more owners jump on board at the time of conversion?

Legal procedures

A sole proprietor can convert his or her one-person business to an LLC in every state. Moreover, a sole proprietor can also bring additional owners into the fray when converting to an LLC. If a sole proprietor decides that the business needs more liability protection or tax protection, then a conversion would make sense. Also, bringing on partners or additional owners would also be a solid reason for converting the business structure. The following requirements are necessary to convert a sole proprietorship to an LLC:

1. **File articles of organization.** The new owners must file LLC articles of organization with the secretary of state filing office.

2. **Prepare an LLC operating agreement.** The new owners should draft an LLC operating agreement explaining ownership interests, profits, losses, voting and liquidation rights, and the other powers and responsibilities of the members. Even a one-member LLC must have an operating agreement, as it also helps to battle aggressive creditors or litigants who seek to pierce the veil of your limited liability and obtain your assets.

3. **Update licenses, permits, and registrations.** The new LLC should obtain new permits, licenses, and registrations in the name of the LLC, and cancel old licenses and permits taken out in the name of the old sole proprietorship. If the LLC is to do business under a name other than that listed in the articles of organization, the owners should file a fictitious name statement.

4. **Obtain an EIN.** A single-owner LLC does not need to obtain an EIN unless the LLC will have employees or establish a retirement plan. Nonetheless, if an LLC consists of more than one individual, the LLC will be treated as a partnership, and an EIN must be retained, even if the LLC has no employees or retirement plan.

Income tax consequences of conversion

The tax effects of changing a sole proprietorship to an LLC are basically identical as for changing a sole proprietorship to a partnership. The IRS and the state tax authorities consider the situation as a change only in the form of business. This same tax-free rule also applies to the creation of a multi-owner LLC, as well as when you bring on additional owners at the time of conversion. The exception to this rule is the same as when a sole proprietorship converts to a partnership — an LLC member who obtains capital (ownership) in an LLC in return for rendering services is taxed on the worth of these services, or the value of his or her ownership share in the business. This occurs even though no cash has exchanged hands in the transaction. Avoid this taxation when you convert to an LLC with new members by:

- Giving the owner who renders services to the LLC an LLC profits-interest only, allowing the owner a share of LLC profits but no voting, liquidation, or other membership rights

- Categorizing the capital contribution of its new member as a know-how contribution of knowledge and development expertise — an intangible piece of personal property that is not taxable

- Buying the interest for cash or a promissory note to pay cash in the future, rather than for rendering services

These tax strategies should be discussed with a tax adviser before implementing them. Ask him or her about other tax exceptions to the rule to be on the safe side.

Tax-filing procedures

Normally, there are no specific tax provisions for sole proprietorships that change over to LLCs. Single-owner LLCs are treated like sole proprietorships insofar as federal income tax reporting and payment. Co-owned LLCs are similar to partnerships. Therefore, changing a sole proprietorship to a one-owner LLC does not change the owner's tax responsibilities. The single LLC owner reports profits and losses on his or her Schedule C, Profit or Loss from Business, as before.

When a sole proprietorship adds new owners and turns into a multi-owner LLC, the new LLC must follow federal partnership tax return rules. It must submit IRS Form 1065 U.S. Return of Partnership Income, and draft a K-1 Partners Share of Income, Credits, Deductions for each LLC member. Members use that information to compile their individual 1040 returns. As with partners, LLC members are not thought of as employees for payroll taxes.

Self-employment taxes

Paying self-employment taxes depends on if the LLC is member-managed or manager-managed. For a brief review, all the owners supervise member-managed LLCs, and manager-managed is where managers are appointed to run the LLC. Under manager-management, one or more individuals have full-time control of the LLC, while the remaining owners are passive investors.

For LLCs that are member-managed, the profits distributed to each member are thought of as earned income, subject to self-employment tax. On the other hand, in a manager-managed LLC, the profits distributed to the managers should be liable for self-employment tax because these managers are active in the business, while profits distributed to nonmanaging members should not be subject to self-employment tax.

Note: "Should" and "should not" are used because there are no clear-cut rules for how members and managers are treated in a manager-managed LLC insofar as the self-employment tax goes. Check with your tax adviser for more details.

Converting a Sole Proprietorship to a Corporation

A sole proprietorship normally converts to a corporation for the benefits unique to the corporate form, such as:

- **Corporate income and tax splitting.** Earnings and profits remaining in the corporation are taxed at corporate tax rates of 15 percent and 25 percent, lower rates than the rates of individual income taxes. If an owner wants to put money back into the business, it is a reasonable decision to incorporate so the retained earnings do not get taxed at the high individual rates.

- **Corporate access to private and public capital.** Incorporating permits you to underwrite common and preferred shares to raise capital with institutional and private investors.

- **Corporate equity-based plans.** Corporations enable you to motivate employees with tax-favored employee stock options, restricted stock bonus and purchase plans, and other plans designed to obtain the best employees.

- **Built-in corporate structure.** If you want to grow your sole proprietorship into a larger business with more of a management structure, then a corporation is for you. State corporation rules and regulations create director, officer, and shareholder positions, each with powers and duties.

There are other ownership issues that might effectuate a conversion from a sole proprietorship to a corporation. For example, an unincorporated business owner may wish to incorporate to form special classes of stock before handing over the reins of control and ownership to the next family generation, or in anticipation of transferring corporate stock to a public buying corporation in a tax-free stock-swap deal.

Legal procedures

A sole proprietorship can convert directly to a corporation. Normally, the sole proprietor transfers the assets and liabilities of the sole proprietorship to the corporation in the

Choosing the Right Legal Form of Business

form of shares, while any added new owners remit cash or property into the corporation in return for shares. Here are the steps:

1. **File articles of incorporation.** Just like creating a new corporation, the sole proprietor must file the articles of incorporation with the secretary of state's office. All states allow one-person corporations.

2. **Select directors and allocate shares.** When a corporation has one owner, only one director is required. If there is more than one shareholder, some states require additional directors; in these states, the amount of shareholders equals the amount of directors. In some states, separate officers must fill separate posts. For example, there must be a separate president and secretary. Check with your secretary of state's Web site to determine your state's requirements.

3. **Draft corporate documentation.** Prepare bylaws and underwrite stock certificates that represent interest in the corporation.

4. **Revise licenses, permits, and registrations.** Update new licenses, permits, and registrations in the name of your new corporation and cancel those under the name of your sole proprietorship. If you are doing business under a name other than the one in your articles of incorporation, file a DBA with your county clerk's office.

5. **Get an EIN.** Get an employee identification number under which you conduct all official business.

You do not need an EIN if you just operate under a sole proprietorship.

Effects of income tax conversion

Normally, you do not have to pay any taxes when converting to a corporation. Nevertheless, the tax-free situation is not automatic. Section 351 of the Internal Revenue Code states that the incorporation is tax-free solely if the new shareholder (or additional shareholders admitted at the time) controls the corporation after the incorporation. By control, we mean that buying shareholders own at least 80 percent of the shares. Look at the following example:

Jack, the sole owner of Jack's Construction, has made the decision to incorporate to limit his personal liability from personal injuries by workers on the site. He transfers all assets and liabilities, which have a net value of $500,000, to the corporation. The company issues Jack 500,000 shares in the corporation for $1 per share. The incorporation act is not taxed under IRC Section 351.

Exceptions to this rule do occur. For example, new shareholders will be taxed on the worth of their stock if they obtain shares in exchange for performing past or future services. This is known as a taxable payment-for-services transaction. In addition, if a shareholder obtains property back from the corporation in addition to shares of stock, the shareholder is responsible for taxes on the fair market value of this property. This is called boot and is taxed by the IRS.

For instance, Lynn transfers the assets of her sole proprietorship worth $100,000 to her new corporation for $25,000 in stock and a $75,000 promissory note, obligating her company to make principal and interest payments to Lynn in return for her transfer of $75,000 worth of assets to the corporation. The IRC 351 rules that they consider the note as income that is taxable to Lynn. Lynn must remit taxes on the $75,000 value of the promissory note, even though she will not receive the money immediately. This is boot income, which has been allotted but not received.

Tax-filing procedures

After you create a corporation, it must pay corporate income tax at corporate rates on its earnings and submit a corporate income tax return, IRS Form 1120, U.S. Corporation Income Tax Return. Once the sole proprietor changes his or her business to a corporation, he or she becomes an employee of the corporation and receives a salary that is also subject to federal and state taxes that are reported on his or her individual income tax return.

The corporation must begin to withhold, deposit, report, and pay payroll taxes for the owner and for any additional employee who comes on board at the time of incorporation and works for the company. This does not translate into more or less social security tax as a corporate employee than as a sole proprietor; it just means that your company will pay one-half of these taxes and, as a corporate employee, you will pay the other half. In essence, both payments come out of your pocket before and after incorporation, so your social security tax amount will be identical. Nonetheless, because corporate profits belong to the owner, the single owner is actually paying the full social security taxes, just as he or she did as a sole proprietor. The money is just coming from two different bank accounts.

Following payroll procedures is a novelty for sole proprietors who did not have employees. The advantage of these procedures is that you do not have to estimate and prepay taxes quarterly as you did as a sole proprietor. The corporation does the withholding for its employees, who include officers, supervisors, staff, and anyone else who renders services for the company.

Converting an LLC to a Corporation

Changing an LLC to a corporation is the most common choice for LLC owners who wish to change business entities. Let us look at the four reasons why business owners would make such a decision:

1. **Corporate income and tax splitting.** If you keep business earnings in the business, corporate income tax rates are 15 percent and 25 percent, which are lower than the rates you would pay on your individual tax return. When you keep income in the business, it makes sense to incorporate to take advantage of these lower tax rates.

2. **Stock.** Incorporating gives owners the opportunity and privilege of underwriting common and preferred stock, which is appealing to investors. Corporations are the business entity of choice for institutional in-

vestors and the public market. Moreover, in family businesses, switching to a corporation allows owners to establish certain classes of stock before handing over the reins of control and ownership to their succeeding generation.

3. **The corporation's equity-based employee plans.** Corporations can attract the finest employees by offering tax-favored stock options, restricted stock bonus and purchase plans, and other equity-based employee incentives.

4. **Corporate structure.** The corporate structure, with its officers and formal regulation, is best suited for larger businesses. It permits for separate management, supervisory, and investment roles. State corporation laws establish separate and distinctive director, officer, and shareholder positions, each with its legal empowerments and responsibilities.

Legal procedures

If you have decided you need to make the move to a corporation for legal or financial reasons, you will need to take the following steps to change your LLC to a corporation:

1. **Look at the state law and terminating provisions of your LLC operating agreement.** Many state laws and most operating agreements necessitate the unanimous consent of all members to dissolve the LLC. Even if it is not stipulated in state law or operating agreement, it is a good idea to get everyone's

approval. Because it affects each member's status as a business owner and taxpayer, each member should examine and approve the change.

2. **Submit the articles of dissolution.** Normally, you submit the articles of dissolution with the state's corporations division or secretary of state's office to terminate an LLC. Many states offer an online form for you to complete, print, and mail to the appropriate government office. It entails filling in the LLC's name and address, date of dissolution, and a description of the membership vote obtained to approve the dissolution.

3. **File articles of incorporation.** The owners must complete and submit articles of incorporation with the proper government office, usually the corporate filing office. Official forms are available online at state corporate filing office Web sites. You file the articles of incorporation together with the required filing fees, normally a flat fee or a fee based on the amount and type of shares authorized in the articles.

4. **Transfer assets and liabilities' underwrite shares.** Normally, the owners of the LLC exchange assets and liabilities from the LLC for shares of stock. The owners usually obtain a percentage of shares in the corporation that is equal to their shares in the original LLC — for example, if four people owned the LLC, each would acquire one-fourth of the shares of stock in the new corporation. If any new owners were brought onboard, such as passive investors, they would have to purchase the shares of stock with cash or property.

5. **Update licenses, permits, and registrations.** The owners should annul any old licenses, permits, and registrations taken out in the name of the old LLC and get new licenses, permits, and registrations in the name of the new corporation. If the corporation is to do business under a name different from the name in the articles of incorporation, you should file with the county clerk or in some states with the corporations division.

6. **Get an EIN.** Obtain an employer identification number even if you do not have employees to include on all business transactions and to open a bank account.

Some states provide for a one-step filing procedure. This document legally dissolves your LLC, creates your corporation, and transfers your assets to the new corporation. This will minimize your paperwork and make the transition easier.

Effects on income tax of conversion

Section 351 of the Internal Revenue Code provides the requirements for a tax-free conversion of an LLC to a corporation. Most conversions are tax-free. Normally, since the IRS treats the single-member LLC as a sole proprietorship, changing the LLC to a corporation is, for tax purposes, identical to changing a sole proprietorship to a corporation. Likewise, since a co-owned LLC is treated as a partnership under the Internal Revenue Code, changing a co-owned LLC to a corporation is identical to converting a partnership to a corporation. Consult a tax adviser to learn of the stipulations of Section 351 of the Internal Revenue Code. He or she should help you adapt your LLC to tax-free standards for conversion to a corporation.

After a business incorporates, each owner who works there becomes a corporate employee. The corporation must withhold, report, and pay payroll and income taxes, including social security and Medicare (FICA). Your corporation pays half of the FICA tax bill and you, as an employee, pay the other half. But, since you own the corporation, you are paying the whole thing — once by the corporation and once out of your own pocket.

Tax-filing procedures

A multi-owned LLC files a final partnership return upon dissolution. A single-owned LLC files a final Form 1040, U.S. Individual Income Tax Return, upon termination. At the time of conversion to a corporation, the former LLC owners will report their corporate salaries as employee wages on their 1040s, which will be taxed at the individual rate. Investors who acquire dividends from the corporation report their earnings on their individual return. Nevertheless, dividend income is presently taxed at a preferential 15 percent in most cases. Once an LLC changes to a corporation, the company files a corporate income tax return, IRS Form 1120, U.S. Corporation Income Tax Return.

Changing an LLC to a Partnership

Although it is not the usual situation, sometimes business owners want to convert their LLCs to partnerships. This occurs when the LLC is legally dissolved, and two or more owners carry out the business. It is uncommon because LLC owners would not want to give up their liability protection and conduct business as an unprotected partnership. Even if the LLC wants new members to join the fold, they would welcome them to their LLC and maintain their limited liability protection rather than convert to a partnership. Nevertheless, perhaps LLC members prefer the decreased paperwork that a partnership requires, or they prefer the less formal structure of a partnership.

Legal procedures

If you have decided to convert your business to a partnership, either because you and a partner want to carry on with the business after your LLC has been dissolved or for other financial or legal reasons, you will need to follow these steps to convert your LLC to a partnership:

1. **Examine termination provisions of your operating agreement.** All members should express their consent to the termination of the LLC. Most LLC operating agreements and many state laws require a unilateral vote of all members to execute dissolution of the LLC. Even when not required by your operating agreement or state law, it is advisable to get each member's approval before dissolving your LLC. As such, it affects each member's legal status as a business owner and taxpayer, so he or she should have a say in the dissolution of the company.

2. **Submit articles of dissolution.** Many states provide a form online for this purpose called articles of dissolution, certificate of dissolution, or articles of termination. You then provide your name and address, date of dissolution, and the nature of the vote taken to dissolve the corporation.

3. **Revise licenses, permits, and registrations.** You should cancel old licenses, permits, and registrations in the name of the old LLC and take out new ones in the name of the new partnership. If the partnership will transact business under a name other than the name of the owners, you should file a new fictitious business name registration form. Sometimes, the states require that you publish a notice of dissolution in the local newspaper. Consult the business section of your local newspaper to determine how you should go about this.

4. **Get an EIN.** Obtain an employer identification number under which you will do business and open a bank account. Even if you do not have employees, you will need this number for tax purposes. Partners are not deemed employees for payroll tax purposes.

Effects on income taxes

Because it is so rare, there are no laws on the books for the tax consequences of converting an LLC to a partnership. The transformation is seen by the IRS as a change in structure only, and not a taxable situation, similar to the conversion of a partnership to an LLC. Nevertheless, if you use the conversion to change ownership, profits, or voting, this may result in a tax termination of the LLC. Consult a financial adviser prior to the conversion even if it is a basic transaction.

Upon dissolution, an LLC must file a final federal partnership tax return, as the IRS considers co-owned LLCs as partnerships. In most states, dissolved LLCs will also have to file final state partnership tax returns. Some states also demand LLCs to file a special LLC tax return. After that, the new partnership then submits an initial partnership tax return to the Internal Revenue Service and to the states to report earnings. When an LLC converts to a partnership, the self-employment tax status of the business owners remains the same. If the owners were active managers of the old LLC, they had to pay self-employment taxes on their share of the earnings. After the change to the partnership, the owners still have to remit self-employment taxes on their share of the earnings.

Changing an LLC to a Sole Proprietorship

It is uncommon to convert an LLC to a sole proprietorship. If the LLC owner does not need legal liability protection anymore or dislikes dealing with the bureaucracy or cost of running the LLC, he or she may dissolve the LLC and convert it to a sole proprietorship. In addition to rare cases such as the California statutory LLC fee scheme, more entry-level taxes may make the LLC an unappealing choice. Furthermore, sometimes a multi-member LLC has one remaining owner. Even in these cases, it is uncommon for the owner to convert his LLC — the remaining member normally keeps the LLC intact. Here is an example:

Bob and Amy own a personal training company, called Fab Abs. They market their services to local corporate businesses. Before long, they have their own niche, with corporate employees calling them for their services. Bob is older and wants to retire, but Amy wants to continue running the business. Amy buys out Bob's interest, and Bob agrees that Amy can continue the business with the same name. Amy decides to stay in business as an LLC instead of a sole proprietorship because she wants to keep the personal liability protection that an LLC provides in case of any sports injuries incurred during the training regimen, such as pulled muscles, due to trainer negligence.

Effect on income tax

Whether you have to pay income taxes after converting an LLC to a sole proprietorship depends on how many members are in the LLC. If a single-owner converts an LLC to a sole proprietorship, there are no federal income tax effects because the IRS treats a single-owner LLC as a sole proprietorship — no change in the tax status of the business has occurred because both before and after the termination of the LLC, profits and losses are reported on individual owner's tax return. Most states also consider a single-owner LLC as a sole proprietorship for state income tax purposes. This signifies that state taxing authorities will not consider the termination or dissolution of a one-person LLC as a taxpaying event for state income tax-paying purposes because it is treated like a sole proprietorship in the first place.

There is an exception to this rule in some states. Where an entity-level tax on LLCs is assessed, the legal termination of the LLC will cause a change in tax treatment. Once the dissolution occurs, the business will not have to remit future LLC entity-level taxes or fees. States that levy an entity-level LLC tax or fee also demand the LLC to submit a final state LLC tax return and get a final LLC state tax clearance stipulating the LLC has paid all outstanding fees and taxes when it submits its legal dissolution papers with the state agency. States that have this regulation may enforce their final tax-filing procedures by demanding that the state corporate filing office wait for the state tax office to issue a final state-LLC tax clearance before submitting the LLC's articles of dissolution.

Under the federal (and most state) law, a co-owned LLC is taxed as a partnership. When the LLC makes a legal change to a sole proprietorship, the tax law considers the change as a tax termination of the partnership. This means that the owners must file a final partnership tax return for the LLC and may owe taxes. After that, the remaining sole proprietor reports earnings of the business on Form 1040 (Schedule C), Profit or Loss from Business, on his or her individual income tax return. If a co-owned LLC drops one or more of its members, it may prefer to change business entities, but it may also want to do business as an LLC. The tax effects of this change are dependent on whether the LLC remains with a single owner or with more than one member. Similarly, a sole owner's LLC is taxed as a sole proprietorship. When a co-owned LLC converts to a single-owner LLC, the IRS will consider it a change from a partnership to a sole proprietorship. The LLC will have to draft a final partnership return, the prior co-owners may have to remit taxes, and the continuing sole owner will begin submitting a Schedule C with his or her individual 1040 tax return where earnings are reported.

If your multi-member LLC drops one or more members but continues to function as a multi-member LLC, you might conjecture that you would not have to pay taxes. Why? You are not changing your LLC to a sole proprietorship, and the IRS still considers your LLC as a partnership. Nonetheless, federal and state tax law may ask you and your co-owners to pay tax when exiting the LLC. Under Section 708 of the Internal Revenue Code, if more than 50 percent of a partnership and its profits change hands during a year, the partnership is ended for tax purposes. This translates into the partnership having to file a final partnership return, with each of the present and past partners owing income tax. Because a co-owned LLC is taxed as a partnership, this tax termination regulation applies to LLCs, too.

For example, Capital Capitalists LLC is a multi-member investment firm with five members, each of whom owns 20 percent of the business. If three of the members exit in a 12-month period, selling their interests back to the LLC or to other members, Section 708 becomes effective because 60 percent of the interests have been transferred during a 12-month period. The LLC must submit a final partnership tax return; the original five members may pay income tax; and the last two members must submit a partnership tax return for the reconstructed LLC.

When the LLC converts to a sole proprietorship, the last owner of the company reports his or her earnings on Form

1040 (Schedule C), Profit or Loss From Business, on an individual tax return. If the previous LLC had one owner, he or she is already reporting his or her income on Schedule C as single-owner. In that case, the new owner need not file any new tax returns. He or she continues to submit a Schedule C where he or she reports profits and pays taxes.

CASE STUDY: FORMING A SINGLE-OWNER S CORPORATION

Robin Kendrick, CPC, President
Physicians Choice Medical Billing
Associates Inc.
748 Sanctuary Cove Drive
North Palm Beach, FL 33410
P: 561-493-7682 F: 561-625-3072
E-mail: pcmedibill@comcast.net

I started my business, Physicians Choice Medical Billing Associates Inc., in August 2005. Currently, I am the only employee. I am trying to obtain one or two large clients so that I can hire someone else to work with me.

Physicians Choice Medical Billing Associates Inc., is a full-service medical billing outsourcing company. We do everything from claim submission to claim follow-up, payment posting, patient billing, and fielding of patient questions. We are able to serve clients in other parts of the country, as most of the communication between Physicians Choice and our clients is via phone, fax, and e-mail. Unlike many of our competitors, we follow up on every claim — even the smallest — and take pride in giving the best and most personal service to our clients. I chose to form an S corporation because I was concerned about protecting my personal assets. I had inquired about an LLC with my ac-countants. It seemed like the S corporation had advantages with regard to the taxation of income. I did not use a lawyer.

I decided to start my own billing business where I could control my environment. In addition, the idea of making my own hours and having that flexibility appealed to me. I also always felt when I was working for others that, "Hey, I think I could do that better." As a result, I ended up starting Physicians Choice and have never looked back. I enjoy what I do, and I do it well.

I recommend consulting either a lawyer or an accountant before starting a business to make sure you understand the differences, benefits, and drawbacks of each of the business formations. There are also other issues. For example, there are strict laws concerning hiring someone as a consultant and paying them on a 1099 rather than as an employee, and there are serious consequences for violating those laws.

The most difficult thing about starting my business continues to be the hardest challenge, and that is marketing. I am a great medical biller but not the best salesperson. I spend a lot of time putting together mailings and doing follow-up phone calls.

I obtained an SBA loan to buy software and my marketing and technical support contracts; however, the interest was really high, at 13 percent. I also realized that I would still need more capital for hardware, marketing, and other things. I was lucky enough to go into the right bank, and a loan officer called me who offered an executive loan that was based on my personal credit. That was what really saved me because I would not have had enough money from the SBA to really get started. The interest on that loan was much more reasonable, too. I would definitely recommend to anyone starting a business that they make sure they have enough starting capital.

The benefits of the S corporation, as I said, are that my personal assets are protected and my income is only taxed once. Although I did not experience a loss with this business, it is not unusual to have that happen in the first year or two, and when that happens — because there is sort of an interface between your personal taxes and the S corporations — you end up with a significant tax return.

Chapter 8
Other Considerations

We have looked at many aspects of starting and operating a business, including legal and tax implications, naming your business, and how to create a marketing and business plan. In this chapter, we will look at other considerations that may affect or be impacted by the legal structure of your business, including location, doing business internationally, and hiring and managing employees.

Operating a Home-based Business

Home-based businesses range in size and complexity. You may be a one-person business with virtually no overhead, or you may have equipment and employees to consider. All home-based businesses face similar challenges regarding time and space management, tax issues, and avoidance of the distractions inherent in working at home.

To help manage some of the challenges involved in managing your physical workspace in a home-based business, be sure to set aside a specific place to work. It should not be near anywhere that papers could catch fire or the family pet could get into your files. Protect your business records and files in plastic storage bins and keep them separate from your personal files and papers. Your workspace should be separate from the kid's play area — if you have one — so that you can concentrate on your work. Consider making adjustments to current living arrangements and whether those changes would incur a cost. Also, ask your family members what they think about your plans.

Be conscientious in your new workspace. You may not be able to dedicate a space in your home and may instead be using a space that is also shared with your family or used for other purposes in addition to your business activities. Consider what is typically in an office and mimic that in your home office. Exercise self-discipline and keep the TV and stereo off, if you cannot remove them completely from your work area. Do not make too many personal phone calls; adhere to your self-imposed deadlines by marking them in a daily planner and checking them off once completed. To maintain a professional image — and to avoid complications involved with using a family phone line — use a separate business telephone line for your home-based business. Set up a quality voicemail system, with a professional outgoing message, to catch calls when you are unavailable. Return your missed calls promptly.

A pamphlet that can be helpful if you are deciding whether a home-based business is your best option is the Small Business Administration publication MP-12 called "Checklist for Going Into Business." It presents the basic steps in gathering information and planning business for home-based business operations. You need to look into the legal and community issues relative to operating a business there before starting your business. There may be restrictions regarding doing business in a residential area that can thwart your plans or would involve expensive renovations to be done to your property before beginning business.

To determine whether your business can be operated out of your home legally, look into the following to be sure you are in compliance:

- Zoning codes

- Permits and licenses

- Deed or lease restrictions

- Parking

- Noise, traffic, and sanitation codes

- Advertising

- State and federal code requirements for space, ventilation, heating, and lighting

- Restrictions on the number and types of workers

- Concerns about what neighbors think of having a business located near them

You learn more about the income tax rules regarding use of a home office by reviewing the Internal Revenue Service Publication #587 Business Use of Your Home.

Doing Business in Other States

If you choose to do business as a LLC or corporation, it leaves you the capacity to allow you to do business out-of-state. Conducting business in another state can have a huge effect on your business. It can determine whether you must register as a foreign (out-of-state) business; it can impact the amount of state income and sales tax you must collect or pay; and it can also affect where your company must go to defend a lawsuit.

If you ignore your business's out-of-state requirements, you may be subject to fines or other legal sanctions. For example, suppose you sue someone in another state and did not register your corporation or LLC in that state. The defendant may petition the court to postpone or drop your lawsuit until you register your corporation or LLC in that state, and remit any late-qualification fees and penalties for late filing. These fees could be significant.

It is apparent how important it is to take care of your out-of-state responsibilities. Therefore, prepare your registration paperwork, pay a qualification fee, and appoint an agent for your company. You may have been tired of the initial work it took to create your LLC or corporation, but if you want to grow your business to other states, it is necessary to deal with the ensuing bureaucracy. The rules for doing business out-of-state for LLCs and corporations are similar. To this extent, this may not be a determining factor in choosing between a LLC and a corporation. However, it is wise to be aware of the rules before choosing either one so you can plan accordingly. The information in this section will be helpful for corporations and limited liability companies that have the following characteristics:

- Form in one state but have its major location in another one

- Form in one state but are situated near the state-lines of other states where it conducts business and/or sells goods or services

- Form in one state but wish to grow nationally or regionally to sell services or products

- Conduct most of or a large portion of business over the Web, by phone, or by mail

State of organization means the state in which you incorporated your business or created your LLC. It would be considered a domestic C corporation or LLC in that state. In every other state that you transact business, it would be considered a foreign LLC or corporation. Foreign does not mean international; it just signifies out-of-state.

Now, let us turn our attention to what "doing business" in another state means. It means, quite simply, that you are registered to do business in your "home" state but want to expand or do business with other states. You will receive business income from another state in addition to the state in which your business is registered to do business. If you are interested in the answer to this question because you want to know if you must register your LLC or corporation and pay taxes and collect taxes, consult the tax laws or codes of that state. The state laws set boundaries for whether a foreign company's transactions are large enough in that state to institute fees or responsibilities on the foreign company. There are rules and standards set by the state's statute that establish when the state can extend beyond its state lines and obtain legal authority over your business's activities and transactions there. The rules for doing business out-of-state or as a foreign entity are normally incredibly similar for LLCs. The differences between them refer to administrative matters, such as the required fees to do business in that state. It remains important, though, to understand what doing out-of-state business entails before you choose either entity. To transact business in another state, you must "qualify" to do business there. Doing business there means where you have a physical presence or perform several business transactions. Mail-order companies and telephone sales businesses do not need to qualify to do business in another state. These companies are exempted from the rule.

Why must LLCs register to qualify to do business as a foreign LLC? The reasons are manifold. First, foreign LLCs must pay for the privilege of doing business in the foreign state. If they are competing against the products and services of the foreign state, the state feels that they should have to pay for that right. Second, the foreign state must offer consumers protection from the LLC doing business there by having a registered agent on call in order to receive legal papers, should a legal suit arise due to, for example, the malfunctioning of a product. Also, the foreign state automatically has jurisdiction over any legal battles against the company to provide further protection for consumers. Carefully consider whether you want to qualify to do business in a foreign state. If you decide to do so, you must file periodic reports there as well as pay taxes. You must also pay a registered agent to receive legal papers.

A foreign or out-of-state company and its owners have to pay state income tax if the business earns money there and the state has income taxes. Besides income tax, sales tax is collected on the purchase of a physical product, such as a consumer product. Normally, sales tax will be collected in a state if a physical personal product is sold and shipped from a physical locale within the state's borders — for example, a retail store or warehouse. As far as defending yourself in a legal action in another state, if your business has qualified to do business there, or if a court determines that you should have qualified to do business there, people may sue you, and you would have to travel to defend yourself in that state. Normally, a company in another state will have jurisdiction over you as a foreign company only if you have a physical existence in the state, produce enough sales from its residents, or advertise regularly in the state.

If you perform Internet sales exclusively, chances are that you will not have to register your company, pay income taxes, or collect sales taxes. Nevertheless, you may still have to show up to defend yourself in another state should a lawsuit arise, particularly if it pertains to the negligence arising out of the sale of your product. Nonetheless, this depends on the type of transaction, income earned from business in that state, and effects of your business activities.

Qualifying

To qualify to do business in another state, there is some paperwork required that comes with its share of fees. Also, you must appoint an agent and follow other rules and laws. This is necessary because states feel that companies must be responsible to their residents both legally and financially if they are doing business there. The reason is that if the company benefits from doing business from their residents, then the residents must benefit from doing business with them. This translates into fees to benefit the state and also the collection of both income and sales taxes. The residents are protected legally by having the right to bring suit upon you and have you defend yourself in their own state courts. This reciprocal relationship is the basis for qualifying to do business in another state.

To understand when you must qualify to do business in another state, you must first understand intrastate business means, which is when at least part of your business is carried out entirely within another state's borders. For example, suppose you incorporated your furniture business in Hempstead, N.Y., and set up an office there, but you also have a warehouse in East Rutherford, N.J., that ships to its residents. This is engaging in intrastate business, and you must qualify to do business in New Jersey and agree to be regulated by its rules and regulations. On the other hand, interstate business — carrying out your business across state lines — does not require qualification to do business or the collection of taxes and fees. For example, your furniture business and its warehouse are both located in Hempstead, and you offer shipping to New Jersey. This is interstate business, and your business does not have to qualify to do business in New Jersey. New Jersey cannot regulate your business nor collect taxes on its profit because, technically, it is not operating within state lines. Each state has rules and regulations governing when businesses must qualify to do business there.

Normally, if your presence in a state is physical — for example, an office or warehouse — or you conduct several and repeated business transactions within the state that are not interstate, such as mail order or telephone sales, this is considered intrastate business, and you must qualify. For example, if you pay employees located in a different state, or rent or possess real estate in a different state, you are most likely conducting business there and must qualify.

In some cases, providing services can be considered intrastate business.

For example, an advertising agency bought airtime for its ads for an auto dealership in Alabama. Although the only physical presence in the state was the ad salesman, the ad agency's business was deemed intrastate because the primary purpose of the contract was the service of broadcasting the advertisements in the local area, according to the judge's decision.

A case-by-case determination is made regarding whether a business is involved with intrastate commerce. When making this decision, the following factors are often considered to be triggers for qualification:

- **Business:** Sales of products or services located within a state — one that does not need the go-ahead from representatives outside the state — frequently require qualification, as do sales made from inventory held there.

- **Work:** If you provide labor or services within the state, you will almost certainly be required to qualify, unless the labor or services are incidental to an interstate sale.

- **Building:** Construction companies located in a different state that employ people and have offices normally must qualify for doing business in that state because they are on-site for several months and do business in that state.

Post-qualification duties

After you are registered or qualified to do business in a state, the state tax authority to collect taxes will contact you. They will send you an annual state income tax return. As a business owner, you must comply with state income and sales tax and also state employment tax filings, if you have a large enough payroll.

In some states, business owners pay a minimum annual corporate income tax. In most states, this figure is less than $100. In other states, such as California or Massachusetts, it is much higher. Also, be aware that if the name of your corporation or LLC in the state you wish to do business in is close to the name of another business on file with the secretary of state, you may be required to change the name of your company or add words to it to make it different. Their list consists of existing corporations and LLCs, as well as foreign corporations and LLCs that are qualified to do business in that state. The secretary of state may also request that you add the terms "LLC" or "Inc." to your name, or incorporate the words "limited liability company" or "corporation" in your name. If the state asks you to choose another name or add words to your existing name to make it different, this new name becomes an assumed or fictitious name, and this will be the name under which you will be required to do business in that state.

Opening branch offices in other states for your corporation and LLC entails all of the responsibilities for foreign corporations for each state you conduct major business in and are involved in intrastate business. That means that for each state in which you have a branch office, you will be required to file the proper paperwork, pay income and sales taxes, pay employment taxes, and pay annual fees in order to keep your business in good standing. In addition, you will be subject to legal action for the maintenance of your business if you should transgress. In some instances, branch offices that have been formed for a limited purpose and participate in certain activities are exempt from qualification according to most state and corporate LLC statutes. For example, if you have a telemarketing company and hire independent contractors to make sales calls in an office in another state, you may not need to qualify to do business in that state. These types of activities are:

- Operating the office or agency for the transmission of the company's own securities.

- Securing sales through independent contractors.

- Getting or trying to get orders (either by mail or via workers or agents) where the orders must be approved outside the foreign state to be closed.

- Conducting meetings of the company's board of directors or shareholders, or conducting other functions regarding the business's internal affairs.

Failing to qualify a business

Failing to qualify a business can result in financial penalties known as late-qualification penalties. For example, according to California law, the penalty is $250 plus $20 per day for willful failure to qualify. This can be costly and add up to substantial sums of money. For example, if the secretary of state in California decides that you willfully conducted business there for two years before qualifying, you could be charged $14,850. Other states assess a flat amount for failure to qualify. Still, these sums could be in the hundreds and even thousands of dollars.

In addition, if you fail to qualify your business out-of-state, you will lose your right to sue in that state's courts. These closed-door statutes entitle the courts to delay or dismiss your lawsuit if the defendant objects on the grounds that you did not qualify your business. Some states will dismiss your lawsuit; others will delay it until you pay your late-qualification fees or qualify your company. Consider the following scenario: A developer whose business is incorporated has an office in Connecticut. He buys land in New Hampshire to build and sell condominiums. He enters into a contract with a New Hampshire contractor to build the condominiums. A disagreement ensued over the contract, and the developer sued the New Hampshire contractor. A court looked over the developer's activities in New Hampshire and found that he was not qualified to do business in New Hampshire. The developer thus was unable to continue with his lawsuit.

When a case is dismissed, you may re-file it within a certain time limit, which may vary with each state, also known as the statute of limitations. First, you must have your business qualified and remit past-due late-qualification fees. If you do not wish to qualify in the foreign state, you can file your lawsuit where your business filed its S corporation or LLC paperwork, but you will have to get jurisdiction over the other business. Bear in mind that not every firm that conducts its activities within a state must qualify to do business there. The rules differ and frequently demand several business transactions, often requiring a physical presence in a state. If your business is conducting interstate commerce (telephone sales, mail order, or sales), you do not have to qualify your business there, and the regulations about delay and dismissal are irrelevant. Let us look at an example to illustrate the point:

A New Hampshire company enters into a contract with a Massachusetts company and conducts intrastate business in the state. Then, the New Hampshire company sues the Massachusetts company. The Massachusetts company claims that the suit is barred because the New Hampshire company failed to qualify to do business in Massachusetts. The Massachusetts court hands down a decision that the New Hampshire company's intrastate business in Vermont was incidental to an interstate purpose. That is, the company's orders were telephone orders and not intrastate business. Therefore, the firm did not need to qualify to do business and is permitted to use the Vermont courts to carry out its lawsuit.

The law protects you even if you failed to qualify when you should have. You always have the right to defend yourself in a lawsuit in another state. Moreover, your contracts are always enforced in that state. Some states incorporate this principle in their long-arm statutes to protect corporations and LLCs. For example, read an excerpt from New York's "Limited Liability Company Law," Section 808, item (b):

> The failure of a foreign limited liability company that is doing business in this state to comply with the provisions of this chapter does not impair the validity of any contract or act of the foreign limited liability company or prevent the foreign limited liability company from defending any action or special proceeding in any court of this state.

Commonly, a state is permitted to stop you from using its courts to bring on a lawsuit if you conduct intrastate business and do not qualify. Moreover, you cannot be sued in a state if you can prove that the state does not have jurisdiction over you according to the state's long-arm statutes. *See the New Hampshire/Massachusetts example above.*

In any case, it is advisable to consult a lawyer or corporation service company to examine the corporate and LLC statutes of the states in which you plan on conducting an incidental amount of intrastate business. If you or your lawyer concludes that your business is intrastate, it is best to pay the modest fees and file the appropriate paperwork with the state so you can use the state's courts to execute your contracts and avoid paying late-qualification fees and penalties. This will save you money in the long run and prevent long delays in court, should you be sued.

Lawsuits in Other States

Suppose you have a corporation located in Michigan. Your secretary has received a summons from a process server. The summons informs you that someone in Alabama has sued you for your company's defective product. However, you have not qualified to do business in Alabama, and you have no office or warehouse there. You want to ignore the summons but are not sure you can. In addition, you want to move the case to Michigan. What should you do?

The issue here is personal jurisdiction and whether the state can hold you to its decision. In other words, personal jurisdiction is what makes the service of process valid and makes the court's decision executable throughout the United States. The law can force you to appear in Alabama (or else incur a default judgment entered against you for not appearing) if your contacts with Alabama bring you within the realm of the state's long-arm statute and meet the constitutionally mandated minimum contacts requirement.

If you agree or consent to defend yourself in a lawsuit, the state will automatically acquire personal jurisdiction. You do this by having a lawyer represent you in court, who files a response to the charges against you. But how do you fight personal jurisdiction? The court permits your attorney to argue the issue of jurisdiction over your company in a special court appearance. If you do not win this fight, further appearances by your lawyer comprise consent to the lawsuit, and the state will have personal jurisdiction over you.

A state's long-arm jurisdiction constitutes whether a non-qualified business in a foreign state must defend itself in case of a lawsuit. Each state has its own long-arm statutes, which explain the situation or circumstances where the state's personal jurisdiction presides over out-of-state companies or individuals. The content of the statutes vary. Some describe activities that comprise a basis for jurisdiction. Others declare that the state has jurisdiction in any circumstance that does not go against the Constitution, delegating the power to the judges to assess activities.

The U.S. Supreme Court has also created a minimum contacts constitutional standard that has to be complied with before a state can demand that an out-of-state company appear in state courts. In this regard, a business must have enough minimum contacts with the state before the business can be coerced to appear and defend itself in court in that state, which is known as the forum state. The state determines contacts as sufficient sales, advertising, or a physical existence — for example, sales agents or officers — in the state in question.

This minimum contacts standard works in conjunction with the state's long-arm statutes to regulate when your company can be forced to defend itself in another state. For example, several long-arm statutes stipulate that the transaction of any business within the state constitutes jurisdiction. This stipulation is then subject to the minimum contacts rule. Your company cannot be required to go to another state for a lawsuit unless the minimum contacts requirement has been met. In this case, it would violate what the Supreme Court has denoted, traditional notions of fair play, and substantial justice.

Take a look at a typical long-arm statute to understand when your company can be forced to defend itself in another state. For example, Michigan's long-arm statute provides for personal jurisdiction over anyone who engages in the following activities:

1. The transaction of any business within the state.

2. The doing or causing any act to be done, or consequences to occur, in the state resulting in an action for tort.

3. The ownership, use, or possession of any real or tangible personal property situated within the state.

4. The contracting to insure any person, property, or risk located within this state at the time of contracting.

5. Entrance into a contract for services to be performed or for materials to be furnished in the state by the defendant.

Practically speaking, personal jurisdiction can be proved by the state over a foreign company that has real property in the state, engages in a tort that results in an injury to one of its residents, or engages in business within the state as stipulated by the minimum contacts requirement. Take a look at these requirements more closely.

Personal jurisdiction relies on the criterion of owning or possessing real property in the state; this is essentially common sense. If you own or lease property in a state, you should be prepared to defend yourself under the jurisdiction of their courts, especially if the dispute arises out of issues derived from the ownership of that property.

Also, states demand that nonresidents who perpetrate torts (a legal case involving damage or injury) show up in court as defendants for that case. For example, someone who throws a rock over the border should be liable for personal jurisdiction in the other state where he or she threw the rock. Examples of tort cases include defamation, invasion of privacy, battery, negligence, and product liability. Another example of when your company may commit a tort in a state: If you pollute a lake or river in a bordering state, you must be prepared to defend yourself from a lawsuit in that nearby state because it is a negligent activity that hurts the other state's residents. Let us now look at the third criterion — transacting business in the state.

Transacting business in the state, even when not qualified to do business there, may still result in jurisdiction, depending on the degree of business being transacted in the forum state. A judge measures the degree of business conducted in a state by examining the following factors:

- **Income within the state.** Courts examine the amount of money your firm earns while doing business in the state. In addition, they consider the percentage of monies earned in that state against your total income. For example, a court will weigh the fact that you earned $50,000 in the state, which is one-quarter of your total income.

- **Physical existence.** Courts examine whether you own or lease real estate or have employees working for you working in that state. If these conditions are met, it is deemed that you have a physical presence in the state and are liable to a lawsuit in that state.

For instance, Cutecats, a New York corporation with an office and store in New York, sells bicycles over the Internet. A Los Angeles resident sues due to a malfunctioning bicycle. Cutecats does one-half of its sales in California, and a judge finds that these sales are enough to constitute jurisdiction in California and requires the New York company to travel to Los Angeles to defend itself against the lawsuit. On the other hand, Cutecats opens a new store in Los Angeles, establishing a physical presence. It is now subject to defend itself against lawsuits in that state regardless of income derived in that state because it has a physical presence in that state.

The issue of minimum contacts is less clear. Legal discussions about it have ensued for more than five decades. Some rules, though, have removed the ambiguity from the discussion. Judges would establish that minimum contacts exist when:

- A manufacturer keeps a store, warehouse, branch office, or some other physical property where the suit originates.

- A business owner from out of state mails catalogs into the state where the suit is originated.

- A lodge advertises to a great extent in the forum state.

- An insurance company hires sales people who seek business over the phone in the originating state of the lawsuit.

- An Internet service provider from out of state trans-acts business with paid customers or takes orders online from subscribers in the state where the law-suit originated.

"Minimum contacts" may sound plural, yet an individual transaction can sanction personal jurisdiction.

For instance, a Texas insurance company sold a single in-surance policy to a California resident. Although this was the only California sale for the Texas insurance company, and they did not even have an officer there, the single sale was enough to force the Texas company to show up in court to defend itself against the charges of the California resi-dent. That is, personal jurisdiction was established, even though it was only one sale and the Texas company did not have an office in California.

Moreover, when a court examines the minimum contacts standard with the forum state, it only takes into consider-ation those contacts the firm made before the charges were brought against them. Jurisdiction rules are often com-plex, and you may not always agree with the judge's deci-sion concerning the sufficiency of your contacts with the forum state. If you have issues about your circumstances or have a legal issue regarding jurisdiction, you may want to seek help from an attorney.

What can you stand to lose if you are sued in another state? You could actually potentially lose everything. Remember, you can only lose something in states that can establish personal jurisdiction over you and that require you to appear to defend yourself. You must have had activities within this state, and the lawsuit must have arisen directly from these activities. For example, if you rent out property in a state and a disagreement results over the lease, the state in which the property is located will have the authority to obtain personal jurisdiction over you, and you will therefore be required to appear in court to defend yourself. Also, if your company is hired to do the plumbing and the work results in damages, you will have to defend yourself in court should any lawsuits arise.

The considerations are cloudier when your firm faces legal action for activities that do not result directly from commerce done in the state. Normally, if your company does business regularly within a state, you must defend all types of lawsuits, even cases that do not directly relate to business conducted there. This is a broad jurisdiction and is called general personal jurisdiction. It is validated by a firm's substantial, continuous, and systematic conduct within the state. Let us look at the following example:

A boat manufacturer, Marsh Company, was incorporated in Florida. While at an Atlanta, Georgia, trade show, Marsh Company made a deal to buy supplies from another company, LPI, and have them shipped to Georgia and North Carolina. Then, a Michigan bank acquired the assets of LPI.

Marsh Company failed to deliver the supplies. A Michigan bank sued Marsh Company in Michigan. Although Marsh Company did not have property or offices in Michigan and did not advertise in Michigan, they did have a sales representative in Michigan and sales of more than $100,000 a year to Michigan residents. Despite the fact that the lawsuit did not result directly from any sales or related matters by Marsh Company in Michigan, and the contract was signed in Atlanta, Marsh is faced with personal jurisdiction in Michigan because the firm's business was substantial, continuous, and systematic.

If you conduct a small amount of business in a state, the likely scenario is that you will only have to appear in court to defend yourself in a smaller range of functions — specifically, those resulting from your doings in the state; this is called limited personal jurisdiction. For example, if your company sells bicycles to state residents, you would only be subject to lawsuits concerning the sale or use of the bikes, not third-party lawsuits such as banks.

Sometimes, provisions within a contract stipulate where lawsuits between the entering parties will take place; these are called forum-selection or jurisdiction clauses. By signing the contract, both parties agree to the jurisdiction of a specific court, thus giving away their right to object to jurisdiction or file a lawsuit in another state. These provisions relate only to issues arising out of the contract itself. For example, if you have a forum-selection provision in a contract in which you agree to supply IT services to a bank, your firm would have to defer to personal jurisdiction over issues resulting from your IT services to the bank specifically. The provision would not cover contracts with other clients unless you included a similar provision, nor would it cover other issues with the bank beside the IT services you provided to them.

Note that two states do not honor these provisions: Idaho and Montana. Some states like Florida ask for additional contact with the disputed company's state beyond the contract that stipulates jurisdiction. Moreover, many state and federal lawsuits do not permit the use of forum-selection paragraphs for certain types of claims. For example, Wisconsin law prohibits forum-selection clauses in contracts to improve land. In that state, they are unenforceable.

When arriving at a decision, a judge will not administer a forum-selection provision in a contract unless it was not signed under coercion, the provision is not illogical, and it does not violate any constitutional criteria. Sometimes, these provisions may be invalid when used in a form contract that a consumer is not likely to read or cannot negotiate. This is called a contract of adhesion. In these cases, what is important is if information about the provision was effectively imparted to the consumer.

For example: A skier purchased a life ticket at a ski slope in Connecticut. The terms of the agreement with the ski slope were on the reverse side of the ticket in fine print; it had a provision that all lawsuits had to take place in Connecticut. The skier fell and hurt himself. He sued in his hometown in the state of New York. The owners of the ski slope objected, declaring the case had to be heard in Connecticut. The New York State court disagreed and stipulated that the forum-selection clause on a ski ticket was not a reasonable method of communicating the information to the skier.

During negotiations, parties often neglect to examine these forum-selection provisions, ignoring them as boilerplate paragraphs. Nevertheless, they should be taken seriously when signing a contract. Let us take a look at another example:

A couple opened up a Jack in the Box franchise in Michigan. In the contract they signed, a forum-selection provision designated Florida as the point of jurisdiction. Problems arose between the franchisor and franchisee, and the couple was informed that they had to show up in Florida to defend themselves in a lawsuit. The couple objected to traveling to Florida and stated that they did not understand the implications of the forum-selection clause. The courts upheld the jurisdiction clause, and they had to appear in Florida to defend themselves or else face a judgment against them.

Forum-selection provisions differ from governing law provisions. Though both are often included in a contract, they stipulate different things. A forum-selection provision establishes where a case can be filed (personal jurisdiction). A governing law clause stipulates which state's laws will be used to determine a decision in the lawsuit. Normally, it is advisable when negotiating a contract to include a forum-selection clause that establishes personal jurisdiction in your state. If you do not have that leverage at the bargaining table, leave out the forum-selection provision entirely. If there is no forum-selection provision, the place where the lawsuit occurs is established by whoever files the lawsuit first.

Which state's laws govern out-of-state disputes? Normally, the laws of the forum state where the lawsuit is filed govern do; nevertheless, this rule may differ according to the nature of the lawsuit and where it originated. In disputes over contracts, some state courts may elect the state with the most prominent relationship to the contract. The selection of a particular state's laws can be important. Suppose you are sued for something where the statute of limitations — or the time frame within which a specific type of case can be filed — has run out in your state, but not in the state where the lawsuit was filed. If you successfully object that your state's laws should take precedence, the lawsuit could not be brought against you because the time limit for filing had expired. Using that argument, you would battle over whether the other state has personal jurisdiction over you.

It is possible to include a provision in your contract, stipulating which state's laws should govern the execution of the contract in the case of a dispute. This is known as a choice of law or governing law provision. Courts normally respect these governing law provisions unless they are determined to be impractical or broach a state statute that forbids their use in specific occurrences. Normally, state laws do not vary with respect to most contract and corporate matters. Nonetheless, some states are focal points for specific industries, and their laws may be more tailored to a specific industry's interests. For example, publishers choose the laws of New York, software and movie firms choose the laws of California, and oil and gas firms like the state laws of Texas and Oklahoma because those states' laws are more business-friendly to those particular indus- tries. If you are unsure of which state's laws are favorable to your industry or firm, consult an attorney when negoti- ating a contract.

Be aware that a choice of law provision can have an influ- ence on whether a court will force you to appear in court in another state to defend yourself in a lawsuit. For example, if you choose California law as your governing law provision, California courts may consider whether the courts in other states have personal jurisdiction over you in California. Af- ter all, if you choose California law, the courts assume you have some connection to California. On the other hand, if a foreign company enters into a contract that includes English law, that would influence the court against estab- lishing personal jurisdiction over the company in a Florida court because its state laws are somewhat different.

Fighting Personal Jurisdiction

Sometimes when you are served with a lawsuit, there are means within your control to have it dismissed and prevent it from going forward based on personal jurisdiction. This, unfortunately, may require much time and expense. It will be necessary to hire an attorney to do the paperwork and file the papers. Attorneys normally file a motion to dismiss order. The argument hinges on the unfairness under the Constitution's due process standards for you to go to the state where the lawsuit was filed to defend yourself there. In essence, you are objecting and stating that the state does not have personal jurisdiction over you.

After you file a motion to dismiss, the court takes two steps in response to it. First, the court examines the state's long-arm statutes to determine whether the state has personal jurisdiction over you. Second, the court examines whether the execution of personal jurisdiction would deprive you and your company of your constitutional right of due process of law. In its examination, the court considers the minimum contacts standard that your company had in the forum state. When the court decides on your case, it will either declare personal jurisdiction, or it will dismiss the case. If you lose the case — that is, if the court establishes personal jurisdiction in which you would have to travel to that state to defend yourself — you can appeal, but this is risky.

At the same time you appeal the jurisdiction case, the initial lawsuit proceeds unless in the rare incident the case is stayed or delayed during the appeal process. Because the case proceeds, and you have not shown up in court, you will receive a default judgment against you. The jurisdiction case is an uphill battle so that you are taking a chance losing the original case by not showing up. If you lose the original case, the plaintiff can start collecting from you in states in which you have tangible assets. It should be noted that appealing a jurisdiction case is costly — it could be more costly than the monies you lose from the original lawsuit. If you ignore the lawsuit brought on by a forum state, a default judgment will be entered against you, and local courts could be summoned to execute the decision against you to collect the judgment monies from your company.

When you start a company, or if you already own one and do business in another state, it is important to understand the distinction between employees and independent contractors. This difference can have a great effect on whether you have the ability to commence a lawsuit against that individual in that state. When you have employees in another state, you normally must qualify to do business in that state, as we have previously discussed. If you employ independent contractors, you are less likely to have to qualify to do business there. For example, if your firm has opened an office with an employee in another state, you would be considered to have conducted intrastate commerce and would have needed to register as a foreign corporation in that state. On the other hand, you are not as likely to be engaged in intrastate business if you hire independent contractors and would not have to register as a foreign corporation. If you do not qualify in a state where you have an employee working for you, you would lose your right to bring a lawsuit against the employee in that state. This may sound like an extreme punishment, but it is not unique.

Take the following as an example: A publishing company in Florida hired a saleswoman who opened up a New York office. The saleswoman got orders for the company and took her commission from the orders she sold. The publishing company had a disagreement with the saleswoman over the amount of commission she collected on behalf of the company. The publishing company sued the saleswoman in New York. The judge ruled in favor of the saleswoman because the publishing company failed to qualify and register the company in New York as a foreign corporation and thus forfeited the right to sue the saleswoman.

When opening up a business, it becomes important to understand whether you want to hire independent contractors or employees. If you hire employees in another state and open up an office for them there, you should qualify to do business there and register to protect yourself. The status of your workers not only is important with regard to do doing business out-of-state, but it is also important in terms of federal income taxes, state unemployment compensation, state income taxes, workers' compensation, overtime, and ownership of intellectual property. Nowadays, many companies are hiring workers on an independent contractor basis to save on the cost of health benefits. Conversely, many individuals are seeking work as independent contractors because of the freedom it offers of working more than one job. When you are a business owner, be aware of the differences.

CASE STUDY: GROWING YOUR BUSINESS

Douglas Dolan
The Solopreneur's Guide
www.thesologuide.com
thesologuide@gmail.com

The mission of my blog, The Solopreneur's Guide, is to help solopreneurs (solo entrepreneurs) create and grow successful, sustainable businesses by navigating them through the building steps of personal introspection, market research, business planning and executing, and business review. I accomplish this mission by providing valuable consulting and copywriting services at reasonable rates, plus timely blog posts discussing current business issues. Although my blog focuses on solopreneurs, I assist other small businesses with my services, too.

I wanted to get started with the blog right away because I am passionate about helping others realize their full business potential, and I knew I could give valuable, free advice right away. Plus, creating the blog gave gave me two benefits: It created an outlet for my need to write, and it created a presence for me on the Internet. I originally started my blog without consulting and copywriting services because I owned and operated another business that I was in the process of selling. During this time, though, I was providing free business advice directly to customers and through various business forums.

I focused on consulting small businesses because it was an excellent mix of my professional experience and personal passions. I took some time for introspection and market research to narrow down and refine my focus before I started The Solopreneur's Guide. I believe that it is possible to create a solo enterprise that is an extension of who you are and what you want in your life, instead of making your life take a backseat to business.

I chose a sole proprietorship because it was the best fit based upon my goals to launch my business quickly with minimal costs. Plus, I have little liability and uncomplicated taxes, so I did not see the need for creating an LLC. My first challenge when starting my business was to find the right focus in a three-month span. Why three months? I was going to put my previous business up for sale and wanted to have something that I could transition to quickly. The second challenge was to create opportunity out of an economy that was in transition from recession to possibly the greatest economic disaster since the Great Depression. I believe that the economy is something to calculate while creating a business plan but should not be the sole, dominant factor.

I drafted 12 points to live by for my business:

1. Create a business that integrates with your life plans of personal and economic goals.

2. Be passionate about your business and the market that you are servicing.

3. Build a business that is an extension of your strengths and experience. Know your weaknesses. Have them covered by others, but manage the results.

4. Research your market (overall industry, competitors, and customers). Make sure that the market is large enough to meet your financial goals, and determine what phase of the S-curve it is in.

5. Have a business plan. Create a plan based upon a unique value proposition for your market at a reasonable price.

6. Make sure that you are well-funded.

7. Get involved within your industry. Build a network of mentors, business associates, and joint venture partners.

8. Know your financial limits. Do not operate beyond your means.

9. Take action. Stay involved. Do not let your business coast on autopilot.

10. Provide a consistent, beneficial experience for your customers.

11. Review your business and market on a regular basis.

12. Make definitive choices and adapt quickly to the changes in your market.

I was able to build credibility by providing references and showing evidence of sound advice through the numerous posts on my blog, along with writing well-received advice on different entrepreneurial forums;

plus, I was offering valuable services at reasonable prices. I typically capture new customers at the point when they hit an obstacle and realize that they need help to get their business moving again.

However, if they sought help earlier, they would have saved more time and money, and dodged most of those obstacles.

I recommend that my customers understand their options when creating a legal entity. I give them an overview of their options to consider but always recommend that they seek the help of professionals: a CPA, a lawyer, or a professional online service (**www.BizFilings.com** or **www. LegalZoom.com**).

Time management and self-discipline are necessary survival skills for the solo-entrepreneur, especially if they operate their business out of their home. It is easy to lose track of focus when the kids are yelling, the dog is barking, the spouse has a question, and someone is ringing the doorbell. To ensure a productive day, I have a few tactics that I recommend.

First, I suggest making a project or to-do list. Second, I break people down into two personality categories: structured and fluid. The structured entrepreneur typically works best when they break the day into defined time periods of specific functions, while the fluid entrepreneur often feels stifled by a structured day. For the structured solopreneur, I recommend that they set a daily schedule of tasks and time buckets. For example, a structured solopreneur operating an online business may have a schedule where each day from 8 a.m. to 9 a.m., he or she reads and answers e-mails; then, from 9 a.m. to 10 a.m., he or she writes a blog post, and so on.

However, using the same example, but inserting a fluid entrepreneur into the equation, I recommend that they create a requirement whereby they will spend one hour each day for e-mails, one hour each day creating content, and so on, but they can complete these time requirements however they want throughout the day, as long as it gets done.

Third, for home-office entrepreneurs, I recommend that they make a firm, formal agreement with their family. It can include appropriate emergency interruptions and scheduled breaks during the day when they will be available; otherwise, they must be left alone. They need to remind their family that if they had to go to work for someone else, they would not have the luxury of allowing the family to stop by or call whenever they want. Working at home is no different. If they want to keep their home-based business, they need to create a firm agreement and resist from enabling interruptions — lock the door, put an "at work" sign on the door, and do not answer questions yelled through the door unless it is an emergency.

When deciding on the appropriate legal entity for your business, ask yourself the following questions:

1. What is the mission of my business, what products and services will I offer, what markets will I service, and what licenses or certifications do I need?

2. What are the different legal business structures that apply to my business?

3. What liabilities do I have for operating my business? Are these high-risk liabilities or low risk? If someone sues me, will I lose my house?

4. What structure offers me the best tax benefits?

Chapter 9
Exit Plans

No business will last forever; every business needs a plan for when it will cease operations. Whether that day comes because of a business failure, buyout, or owner retirement, you must have an exit plan developed even before you start your business. Your exit plan should be written into your business plan so that if something does happen that you had not expected, you or your successors will have a clearer understanding of how the situation will be handled. In this chapter, we will look at the ways a business could end or cease to exist in its current form; the implications for the business owner, successors, and beneficiaries; and how to legally handle certain situations.

Why You Need an Exit Plan

One thing that far too many do not realize is that when they die, and they do not have a specific exit strategy for their business — which includes paying off their debts and leaving money for their family — they are leaving them open to disaster. Any debt the business has created, which otherwise would be paid off as the business venture continues, would fall on the family should you die. Because most families would not have the ability to take over the business, they are forced to liquidate its assets to close any debt the business has incurred. There are many stories of millionaire entrepreneurs whose fortunes were quickly lost within a few years after they died because of poor planning. Joe Robbie, original owner of the Miami Dolphins, is one such story.

In 1990, Robbie died unexpectedly at age 73, leaving his family without an exit plan for his business entities and what would happen with them. The family was forced to auction off much of his estate. Robbie's business planning was unfortunately incomplete because he did not include what to do about estate taxes, which resulted in his family's being left with a reported $47 million in estate taxes. Over the next four years, his family's net worth dissolved, leaving them with what appeared to be no other alternative than to sell the one thing of value left in their possession: the Miami Dolphins and the Joe Robbie Stadium (now Pro Player Stadium). They sold these assets for $138 million — a fraction of its value — in order to cover the estate taxes, in effect losing the assets and the ability to continue Robbie's intended legacy. As of 2008, the value of the Miami Dolphins is estimated at $1 billion, according to Forbes.com.

The Robbie story highlights a simple fact: This type of financial fiasco can be easily avoided with proper, thorough planning. Robbie put up private funds to launch his dream, earned it back, and created a vast estate, but that earned business money was not protected in any way, leaving it open to estate taxes. You will have to ask yourself if the risk is worth the possible outcome of leaving your family with nothing, or the liquidation of your business efforts.

Dissolving and Liquidating a Corporation

The owners of a small corporation may arrive at a decision to shut down business and pursue other options. To accomplish this, the owners dissolve and liquidate the corporation by selling its assets, allocating the cash proceeds to creditors and shareholders, and submitting official dissolution paperwork to the state office. To dissolve a corporation, its owners must draft and submit articles of dissolution or a certificate of dissolution. As part of the state dissolution procedure, the corporation must remit any outstanding state corporation income tax and offer payment to creditors of the business. The corporation then can allocate any leftover assets to shareholders in proportion to their stock interests. A notice of dissolution normally must be published in a legal newspaper and shareholders and creditors can usually ask a court to supervise the dissolution procedure to ensure it goes smoothly and is in compliance with the state's laws governing corporations.

Effects on income tax of dissolution

Upon a corporation's dissolution, it must submit final state and federal income tax returns and remit any outstanding taxes due. The shareholders and corporation may both owe taxes. For example, the corporation may owe income tax if its assets grew during its existence, or if the corporation has to recoup depreciation previously taken on its liquidated assets. The shareholders may also owe taxes if the amount of cash or value of property they acquire on liquidation is more than their individual income tax basis in their shares. Sometimes, special tax breaks are offered when one corporation is sold to another corporation as part of a tax-free reorganization. At dissolution, corporation owners must also submit final federal and state payroll tax returns and remit all final social security and Medicare tax deposits for their employees and themselves.

Instead of closing the doors of their businesses, corporations often are bought by other businesses, and these purchases have vital tax and legal consequences. The process of selling a corporation falls into one of two categories: In one situation, the buyer desires the corporation's assets (for example, the brand and other intangible assets) but does not want to conduct the corporation's business. In this case, the corporation dissolves. In the second situation, the buyer purchases the stock of the corporation to continue to run the business. In this case, the corporation remains alive and does not legally dissolve, but shareholders and management could potentially change.

Sale of assets

An asset sale affects the legal dissolution of a corporation, and for C corporations, both shareholders and the corporation may have taxes due. The tax pertains not only to the sale of tangible assets but also to its intangible assets, such as goodwill. Goodwill involves the attractiveness of the business and its assets to the buyer, namely its reputation, brand, future sales, and growth potential. It is usually configured as the amount by which the sale price of the corporation goes over the fair market value of its assets. Goodwill is an intangible asset, but it is also liable to corporate-level and shareholder-level taxes when the sale of the corporation is made.

In an asset sale, the buyer gets a stepped-up tax basis in the bought assets equal to the figure of the purchase price allocated to each asset. A stepped-up tax basis allows the buyer to take greater sums of depreciation on depreciable assets after the purchase, which can lower taxes. The purchase price in an asset sale must be distributed between physical assets and goodwill. This distribution has tax consequences for both the seller and the buyer — for example, the distribution can influence how much depreciation the buyer takes later on the assets purchased. The rules are complex, so consult a tax adviser.

In addition, buyers may choose an asset sale because by buying the assets instead of the stock of the corporation, the buyer avoids successor liability, which occurs when the buyer in a corporate stock sale becomes liable for claims — such as from debtors or for liability issues — made against the selling corporation after the sale. A seller may indemnify the buyer against such legal claims, even going to the extent of putting money in an account to pay for them. Nonetheless, that is why buyers often prefer to engage in asset sales: so they can avoid the situation entirely.

Selling stock

The corporation does not dissolve in a normal stock sale. It continues its existence as a corporate entity; it is just under the new managers. The new owners vote for a new board to take over management, and this new board elects new officers. In this buy-out event, only the shareholders benefiting from the sale — not the corporation — owe taxes on the stock transaction. Each shareholder pays capital gains taxes on the figure by which the sales price is more than the shareholder's basis in his or her shares. Owners of corporations normally prefer to sell their stock rather than the assets because a stock sale ends in only one level of tax to the shareholders — the proceeds from the sale are not decreased by corporate-level tax liability.

A corporation-to-corporation sale

Sometimes, a C corporation sells its stock or assets to another C corporation in exchange for its stock and cash. This transaction is known as reorganization, which differs from the conversion of a corporation into another entity such as a sole proprietorship, LLC, partnership, or a sole proprietorship — the corporation merely converts to a new corporation.

Reorganizations that adhere to tax rules and the tax codes of states are entitled to tax-free treatment in the selling and buying of corporations. There are a number of ways to acquire this tax-free treatment, but the laws are complicated, so consult a tax adviser to get it right. These reorganization tax rules benefit only corporations, not unincorporated businesses. You must possess a corporation and sell it to another corporation to be entitled to this tax advantage.

Types of Reorganizations

Merger and non-merger are the two types of reorganizations. Let us look at each of them.

Merger reorganizations: In this type of reorganization, a buying corporation purchases the stock of a selling corporation. On dissolution of the sold corporation, the assets and liabilities are transferred to the buying corporation. The merger reorganization provides the advantage of a minimum amount of paperwork, as the transfer of assets and liabilities happens automatically. This liquidation and dissolution occurs smoothly when one corporation merges with another. The seller need not submit special forms to the state.

Non-merger reorganizations: Several types of non-merger reorganizations exist. For example, an exchange reorganization happens when a selling corporation sells the majority of its shares to another corporation in exchange for its shares. A sale of assets reorganization happens when a selling corporation's shares are sold to another corporation in return for the buyer's shares. Unlike a merger, an exchange or sale of assets reorganization does not involve the liquidation of the selling corporation and legal merger into the buying corporation.

Reorganization procedures

Generally, the board of directors and the shareholders of both the buying and selling corporation must approve a plan of merger or reorganization. Normally, at least a majority of the shareholders who have the right to vote (often two-thirds) must approve the plan.

Dissenters of the plan — shareholders who oppose the sale but do not have enough votes to stop it — acquire dissenters' rights. For example, a state may offer that if 5 percent or more of the shareholders oppose it, all dissenters can demand the selling corporation buy back their shares at the fair market value rather than having to exchange them for shares of the buying corporation. If the corporation fights the dissenting shareholders' requests for a buy-back, the dissenters can sue the corporation in state court. If the shares are traded on a national stock exchange, dissenters normally do not acquire buy-back rights because they can normally sell their shares on the stock exchange.

Each state offers its own forms and procedures for executing corporate mergers and other reorganizations. These forms are normally available on the state corporate filing office's Web site. Certificates of merger and other reorganization forms normally demand that the filer has met all legal requirements for a corporate merger or other reorganization. Simply attach a copy of the merger or other reorganization agreement or plan to the document filed. Moreover, states that have an income tax normally require that the corporation that is merging with another corporation acquire a final clearance from the taxing authorities, declaring that all corporate income or franchise taxes have been paid, before the date the merger is to take place.

Effects on income tax of corporate reorganizations

The selling and buying corporations do not remit tax on the transaction of a tax-free reorganization. In lieu of that, the buying corporation inherits the assets and liabilities of the selling corporation, and the tax obligations relative to these assets. For example, the selling corporation's basis in each asset is transferred and becomes the buying corporation's equivalent in those assets. Consequently, tax on the sale of the transferred assets is delayed until the buying corporation sells the assets to another corporation in a sale that is taxed.

Normally, in a tax-free Type A reorganization, named after IRC Section 368(a)(1)(A) of the Internal Revenue Code, the shareholders can acquire cash and stock in the buying corporation in exchange for the sale of their shares in the selling corporation. When the shareholders receive stock only, there is no taxation involved. In lieu of this, they receive a basis in the new shares equal to the basis in the old shares. When they sell their new shares, the shareholders pay capital gains tax on the amount greater than the carried-over basis in the new shares.

When a shareholder in a Type A reorganization acquires cash for his or her shares from the buying corporation, any amount that is greater than the shareholder's stake in the shares will be taxed at capital gains rates. The IRS allows for the buying corporation in a Type A reorganization to pay up to one-half of the purchase price in cash and one-half in its shares when it buys out the shareholders of the selling corporation without sacrificing the tax-free aspect of the deal. Many tax professionals consider it possible to have an even larger ratio of cash-to-shares in the buyout — for example, from 55 percent to 60 percent in cash and only 45 percent to 40 percent in the selling corporation's stock — and still meet the requirements for a tax-free reorganization.

Dissolving a Partnership

If your partner dies or you buy out your partner, perhaps because the partnership is no longer working out for one or both of you, your partnership would become a sole proprietorship. If you and your partner operated a consulting business but your partner wanted out of the business for whatever reason, you would dissolve the partnership and become a sole proprietorship.

It is not necessary to file any paperwork to change your partnership to a sole proprietorship. However, if you had formed a limited partnership or if you were completed closing the business, you would have to file formal papers with the state's filing office to dissolve it. The first step in dissolving the partnership is to determine the assets and each partner's share.

The dissolution of a partnership results in a taxable gain or loss to the ex-partners, even if it turns into a sole proprietorship. Section 708 of the Internal Revenue Code considers the transfer of 50 percent or more of the parts in a partnership (or LLC) as a tax termination of a partnership. What that means is that if half of the partnerships' interests are sold or liquidated, the partnership is considered dissolved and each owner may be liable for taxes.

When dissolving your partnership, determine how much of the assets each partner is entitled to. Taxes will have to be paid on any gains either partner realizes from the sale of assets and from the distribution of assets on the dissolution. Each partner will also be responsible for his or her share of the debts incurred by the business. Dissolution also involves submitting paperwork with your state, which may be a simple form indicating that the business has been dissolved, depending on the state. The partnership should then send a final Form 1065, U.S. Partnership Return of Income and also complete final K-1s (Partner's Share of Income Credits, Deductions, etc.) for the ex-partners.

Dissolution of an LLC

When the life of an LLC comes to an end, it is known as dissolution, which means physically shutting down of an LLC, sorting out its affairs, paying its creditors, apportioning its assets to shareholders, and essentially ending its life. There are three types of dissolution:

- **Voluntary dissolution** occurs when the management intentionally shuts down the LLC.

- **Administrative dissolution** occurs when the secretary of state or other official agency orders it closed.

- **Judicial dissolution** is a court-ordered dissolution of the company.

A voluntary dissolution may be voted on by a meeting of the members or by written consent. Members then file a notice of dissolution or application for dissolution with the secretary of state. The secretary of state may not approve dissolution for an LLC that is not in good standing or owes an outstanding tax liability.

The secretary of state has the power to order an LLC's administrative dissolution. The secretary of state may exercise this power when an LLC fails to file its periodic reports or tax reports. The criteria for what is exactly delinquent enough to order an administrative dissolution varies from state to state. Some states offer a reinstatement of good standing after an administrative dissolution once the LLC files the periodic reports, pays taxes, or complies with the state's requirements to obtain a reinstatement. In such cases, a penalty is usually levied.

A court may order the judicial dissolution of an LLC. This would be executed upon the request of an attorney general, LLC owner, or creditor. For example, a member may sue to dissolve an LLC when the LLC is wasting assets to the member's dismay, when members are violating the other member's rights, or if there is a tie in voting. Always try to avoid dissolution of an LLC; it can lead to a failure of liability protection. Also, never dissolve an LLC in debt. If you do, you may be personally responsible for the debt.

When dissolving the LLC, you will need to determine each person's stake in the LLC and the value of the entity's assets. Then you must file IRS Form 966, in addition to a number of filings to your state office, as what is required specifically varies by state. You will need to send a notice to any creditors, which gives information on where to send their claims and how to process all creditor claims.

CASE STUDY: DO YOUR OWN RESEARCH

Michael Ferreira, President & Founder
MFRisk Solutions, LLC
PO Box 90562
Staten Island, NY 10309-0562
Michael.Ferreira@mfrisksolutions.com

My business focuses on risk management consulting for entrepreneurs, solopreneurs, start-ups, and insurance agents. With 16.5 million Americans unemployed (and this number will grow before press time), many people are pursuing their dream of beginning their own businesses. I have met a large number of people who are "subject matter" experts who have worked in a corporate environment and now want to leverage that experience and knowledge on their own behalf. Technical knowledge alone will not guarantee success. I consult with people on the risks they face starting a business and develop plans to address those risks.

When I formed my own business, I chose to structure it as an LLC. Though I am the sole proprietor, I anticipate my business growing and the need for other partners or investors. The organization is now structured to accommodate growth. When planning and starting up my business, I was unprepared for the amount of research it would take just to start the business. I had to develop plans and strategies for establishing the business, marketing, advertising, building a Web site, and networking.

For others considering starting a business, I would advise you to try to do as much as possible on your own. Most research can be done for free. By tackling some of the issues on your own, you become a better-informed business owner and leader. This way, when you increase your dependency on advisers or service providers, such as lawyers or accountants, you will be better informed and will be an efficient procurement person.

Conclusion

As an aspiring new business owner, you have a lot of decisions to make. You will first need to decide what type of business to start and operate, then decide what you will call your new business. Furthermore, you will also need to investigate options for where your business will operate. This is a particularly important decision if you are considering a home-based business, as it will affect your family life as well. But of all the considerations you must weigh when starting your business, the choice of which legal entity may well be the most important.

The decision to operate as a sole proprietor, C corporation, or to go with some option in between must be made only after careful deliberation and considerable research. You have taken the first step by reading through the information provided in this book. You should follow up by investigating the specific requirements of your state. You can check the state's Web site. *See the Appendix for these URLs.* You might also consider consulting with your local Small Business Administration office. *A list of the state SBA offices is also provided in the Appendix.*

Although many aspiring entrepreneurs base their decisions on what they can afford to do at the time, the cost of forming certain types of legal business entities should not be the only consideration involved. Often, paying a little more now can help protect you (and save you money) as your business grows. Review your business idea, including the location you have chosen, to determine what type of liability you might face in your business operations. If you have a consulting business with little overhead and virtually no liability potential, you probably do not need the protection afforded by the more expensive options.

Forming a corporation may seem daunting to someone considering launching a business. In many ways, the legal and tax requirements can become overwhelming. If you have examined your business idea thoroughly and are convinced a corporation is the best structure given your circumstances, it will certainly be worth the investment on your part to bring in professional assistance to guide you through the paperwork. Failing to file certain paperwork, initially and throughout the life of the corporation, can result in serious consequences for both you and your business.

As with all aspects of planning and launching your business, consider your decision regarding the legal form of your business with great care. With meticulous research and preparation, you and your business can be successful.

Appendix

State Web Sites and SBA Offices

You will need to register your business name with your state authority, usually at the secretary of state's office. Most states provide online information on their requirements, as well as an online form for you to submit along with the appropriate fee. The following lists the Web sites for each state to help you begin the process of registering and naming your business.

Alabama
www.sos.state.al.us

Alaska
www.commerce.state.ak.us

Arizona
www.azsos.gov/business_services

Arkansas
www.state.ar.us/business_res.php

California
www.calbusiness.ca.gov/default.asp

Colorado
www.colorado.gov/cbe

Connecticut
www.cga.ct.gov

Delaware
www.delaware.gov

Florida
www.dos.state.fl.us

Georgia
www.legis.state.ga.us

Massachusetts
www.mass.gov

Hawaii
www.hawaii.gov

Michigan
www.legislature.mi.gov

Idaho
www.sos.idaho.gov

Minnesota
www.sos.state.mn.us

Illinois
www.ilga.gov

Mississippi
www.mscode.com

Indiana
www.state.in.us

Missouri
www.sos.mo.gov

Iowa
www.legis.state.ia.us

Montana
http://sos.state.mt.us

Kansas
www.kssos.org

Nebraska
www.sos.state.ne.us

Kentucky
www.lrc.state.ky.us

Nevada
www.sos.state.nv.us

Louisiana
www.sec.state.la.us

New Hampshire
www.sos.nh.gov

Maine
www.maine.gov/sos

New Jersey
www.njleg.state.nj.us

Maryland
www.dat.state.md.us

New Mexico
www.sos.state.nm.us

New York
www.dos.state.ny.us

North Carolina
www.ncga.state.nc.us

North Dakota
www.nd.us

Ohio
www.sos.state.oh.us

Oklahoma
www.sos.state.ok.us

Oregon
www.filinginoregon.com

Pennsylvania
www.dos.state.pa.us

Rhode Island
www.state.ri.us

South Carolina
www.scstatehouse.net

South Dakota
www.state.sd.us

Tennessee
www.state.tn.us/sos

Texas
www.sos.state.tx.us

Utah
www.commerce.utah.gov

Vermont
www.leg.state.vt.us

Virginia
www.virginia.gov

Washington
www.dol.wa.gov

West Virginia
www.wvsos.com

Wisconsin
www.sos.state.wi.us

Wyoming
soswy.state.wy.us

Small Business Administration (SBA) Offices

When you are considering starting your own business, contact your state's SBA office to get more information about its counseling and loan services. Many SBA services are provided at no charge, including online resources and guidance available on their Web site at **www.sba.gov.**

Alabama District Office
801 Tom Martin Drive,
Suite 201
Birmingham, AL 35211
Phone: (205) 290-7101
Fax: (205) 290-7404

Alaska District Office
510 L St., Suite 310
Anchorage, AK 99501
Phone: (907) 271-4022
Fax: (907) 271-4545

Arizona District Office
2828 North Central Ave.,
Suite 800
Phoenix, AZ 85004
Phone: (602) 745-7200
Fax: (602) 745-7210

Arkansas District Office
2120 Riverfront Drive,
Suite 250
Little Rock, AR 72202

Phone: (501) 324-7379
Fax: (501) 324-7394

California — Los Angeles District Office
330 North Brand,
Suite 1200
Glendale, CA 91203
Phone: (818) 552-3215
Fax: (818) 552-3286

California — Sacramento District Office
6501 Sylvan Rd., Suite 100
Citrus Height, CA 95610
Phone: (916) 735-1700
Fax: (916) 735-1719

California — San Francisco District Office
455 Market St., 6th Floor
San Francisco, CA 94105
Phone: (415) 744-6820
Fax: (415) 744-2119

Colorado District Office
721 19th St., Suite 426
Denver, CO 80202
Phone: (303) 844-2607
Fax: (303) 844¬-6468

Connecticut District Office
330 Main St., 2nd Floor
Hartford, CT 06106
Phone: (860) 240-4700
Fax: (860) 240-4659

Delaware District Office
1007 N. Orange St., Suite 1120
Wilmington, DE 19801
Phone: (302) 573-6294
Fax: (302) 573-6060

Florida — Jacksonville District Office
7825 Baymeadows Way, Suite 100B
Jacksonville, FL 32256
Phone: (904) 443-1900
Fax: (904) 443-1980

Florida — Miami District Office
100 S. Biscayne Blvd., 7th Floor

Miami, FL 33131
Phone: (305) 536-5521
Fax: (305) 536-5058

Georgia District Office
233 Peachtree St. NE, Suite 1900
Atlanta, GA 30303
Phone: (404) 331-0100
Fax: (404) 331-0101

Hawaii District Office
300 Ala Moana Blvd., Room 2-235
Honolulu, HI 96850
Phone: (808) 541-2990
Fax: (808) 541-2976

Idaho District Office
380 E. Parkcenter Blvd., Suite 330
Boise, ID 83706
Phone: (208) 334-1696
Fax: (208) 334-9353

Illinois District Office
500 W. Madison St., Suite 1250
Chicago, IL 60661
Phone: (312) 353-4528
Fax: (312) 886-5688

Indiana District Office
8500 Keystone Crossing,
Suite 400
Indianapolis, IN 46240
Phone: (317) 226-7272
Fax: (317) 226-7259

Iowa District Office
210 Walnut St., Room 749
Des Moines, IA 50309
Phone: (515) 284-4422
Fax: (202) 481-5838

Kansas District Office
271 W. 3rd St., Suite 2500
Wichita, KS 67202
Phone: (316) 269-6616
Fax: (316) 269-6499

Kentucky District Office
600 Martin Luther King Jr.
Place, Room 188
Louisville, KY 40202
Phone: (502) 582-5971
Fax: (502) 582-5004

Louisiana District Office
365 Canal St., Suite 2820
New Orleans, LA 70130
Phone: (504) 589-6685
Fax: (504) 589-2339

Maine District Office
68 Sewall St., Room 512
Augusta, ME 04330
Phone: (207) 622-8551
Fax: (207) 622-8277

Michigan District Office
477 Michigan Ave.,
Suite 515
Detroit, MI 48226
Phone: (313) 226-6075
Fax: (313) 226-4769

Minnesota District Office
100 N. 6th St., Suite 210-C
Minneapolis, MN 55403
Phone: (612) 370-2324
Fax: (612) 370-2303

Mississippi District Office
Regions Plaza
210 E. Capitol St.,
Suite 900
Jackson, MS 39201
Phone: (601) 965-4378
Fax: (601) 965-5629

Maryland District Office
City Crescent Building
10 S. Howard St., 6th Floor
Baltimore, MD 21201

Phone: (410) 962-6195
Fax: (410) 962-1805

Massachusetts — Boston District Office
10 Causeway St.,
Room 265
Boston, MA 02222
Phone: (617) 565-5590
Fax: (617) 565-5598

Missouri — St. Louis District Office
200 North Broadway,
Suite 1500
St. Louis, MO 63102
Phone: (314) 539-6600
Fax: (314) 539-3785

Montana District Office
10 West 15th St.,
Suite 1100
Helena, MT 59626
Phone: (406) 441-1081
Fax: (406) 441-1090

Nebraska District Office
10675 Bedford Ave., Suite 100
Omaha, NE 68134
Phone: (402) 221-4691
Fax: (402) 221-3680

Nevada District Office
400 South 4th St.,
Suite 250
Las Vegas, NV 89101
Phone: (702) 388-6611
Fax: (702) 388-6469

New Hampshire District Office
JC Cleveland Federal Building
55 Pleasant St., Suite 3101
Concord, NH 03301
Phone: (603) 225-1400
Fax: (603) 225-1409

New Jersey District Office
2 Gateway Center,
15th Floor
Newark, NJ 07102
Phone: (973) 645-2434
Fax: (973) 645-6265

New Mexico District Office
625 Silver SW, Suite 320
Albuquerque, NM 87102
Phone: (505) 248-8225
Fax: (505) 248-8246

New York District Office
26 Federal Plaza,
Suite 3100

New York, NY 10278
Phone: (212) 264-4354
Fax: (212) 264-4963

**New York — Buffalo
District Office**
Niagara Center
130 S. Elmwood Ave.,
Suite 540
Buffalo, NY 14202
Phone: (716) 551-4301
Fax: (716) 551-4418

**New York — Syracuse
District Office**
401 S. Salina St., 5th Floor
Syracuse, NY 13202
Phone: (315) 471-9393
Fax: (315) 471-9288

**North Carolina District
Office**
6302 Fairview Rd.,
Suite 300
Charlotte, NC 28210
Phone: (704) 344-6563
Fax: (704) 344-6769

**North Dakota District
Office**
657 2nd Ave. North,
Room 218

P.O. Box 3086
Fargo, ND 58108
Phone: (701) 239-5131
Fax: (701) 239-5645

**Ohio — Columbus
District Office**
401 N. Front St., Suite 200
Columbus, OH 43215
Phone: (614) 469-6860
Fax: (614) 469-2391

Oklahoma District Office
301 NW 6th St.
Oklahoma City, OK 73102
Phone: (405) 609-8000
Fax: (405) 609-8990

Oregon District Office
601 SW 2nd Ave., Suite 950
Portland, OR 97204
Phone: (503) 326-2682
Fax: (503) 326-2808

**Pennsylvania — Philadel-
phia District Office**
Parkview Tower
1150 1st Ave., Suite 1001
King of Prussia, PA 19406
Phone: (610) 382-3062
Fax: (202) 481-6469

Pennsylvania — Pittsburgh District Office
411 7th Ave., Suite 1450
Pittsburgh, PA 15219
Phone: (412) 395-6560
Fax: (202) 292-3771

Rhode Island District Office
380 Westminster St.,
Room 511
Providence, RI 02903
Phone: (401) 528-4561
Fax: (401) 528-4539

South Carolina District Office
1835 Assembly St.,
Room 1425
Columbia, SC 29201
Phone: (803) 765-5377
Fax: (803) 765-5962

South Dakota District Office
2329 N. Career Ave.,
Suite 105
Sioux Falls, SD 57107
Phone: (605) 330-4243
Fax: (605) 330-4215

Tennessee District Office
50 Vantage Way, Suite 201
Nashville, TN 37228
Phone: (615) 736-5881
Fax: (615) 736-7232

Texas — Dallas/Fort Worth District Office
4300 Amon Carter Blvd.,
Suite 114
Fort Worth, TX 6155
Phone: (817) 684-5500
Fax: (817) 684-5516

Utah District Office
125 South State St.,
Room 2227
Salt Lake City, UT 84138
Phone: (801) 524-3209
Fax: (801) 524-4160

Vermont District Office
87 State St., Room 205
Montpelier, VT 05601
Phone: (802) 828-4422
Fax: (802) 828-4485

Virginia District Office
400 North 8th St.,
Suite 1150
Richmond, VA 23219
Phone: (804) 771-2400
Fax: (804) 771-2764

Washington District Office
2401 4th Ave., Suite 450
Seattle, WA 98121
Phone: (206) 553-7310
Fax: (206) 553-7066

Washington D.C. District Office
Metropolitan Area
740 15th St. NW, Suite 300
Washington, DC 20005
Phone: (202) 272-0345
Fax: (202) 606-4225

West Virginia District Office
320 W. Pike St., Suite 330
Clarksburg, WV 26301
Phone: (304) 623-5631
Fax: (304) 558-2539

Wisconsin District Office
740 Regent St., Suite 100
Madison, WI 53715
Phone: (608) 441-5263
Fax: (608) 441-5541

Wyoming District Office
100 E. B St., Room 4001
Casper, WY 82602
Phone: (307) 261-6500
Fax: (307) 686-5792

Bibliography

Mancuso, Anthony. *LLC or Corporation? How to Choose the Right Form of Business*. Berkeley, CA: Nolo Press, 2006.

Mancuso, Anthony. *Nolo's Quick LLC*. Berkeley, CA: Nolo Press, 2007.

Piper, Mike. *Surprisingly Simple. Independent Contractor, Sole Proprietor, and LLC Taxes Explained in 100 Pages or Less*. Chicago: Simple Subjects, LLC, 2009.

Sitarz, Daniel. *Sole Proprietorship Small Business Start-up Kit*. Carbondale, IL: Nova Publishing Company, 2005.

Spadaccini, Michael. *Entrepreneur Magazine's Ultimate Book on Forming: Corporations, LLCs, Sole Proprietorships, and Partnerships*. Canada: Entrepreneur Press, 2004.

Author Biography

PK Fontana is a freelance writer and trainer, specializing in business communications and entrepreneurial topics. Based in Cary, North Carolina, her clients include businesses and individuals from across the country. She has earned a master's in English with a concentration in technical and professional communications from East Carolina University, and she plans to continue teaching at the community college level, helping students develop professional writing skills before they enter the workforce or start their own businesses. PK is married, the mother of two, and the stepmother of four. She grew up on the beaches of the Gulf Coast of Florida and plans to eventually retire on the beach of the Jersey Shore. Learn more about PK's writing and training at **www.pkwriting.com**.

Index

H

I

J

L

M

N